I0491594

Mosques of

Morocco

مساجد المغرب

Coffee
Table
Photobook

Mosaic Tree Press

ISBN 978-1-916524-83-5

All artwork was designed and licensed by freepik.com & Unsplash.com

First printing, 2024

Published by Mosaic Tree Press
Browse our complete catalogue of publications at MosaicTree.org

Published by

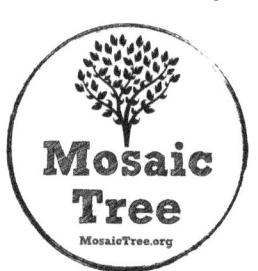

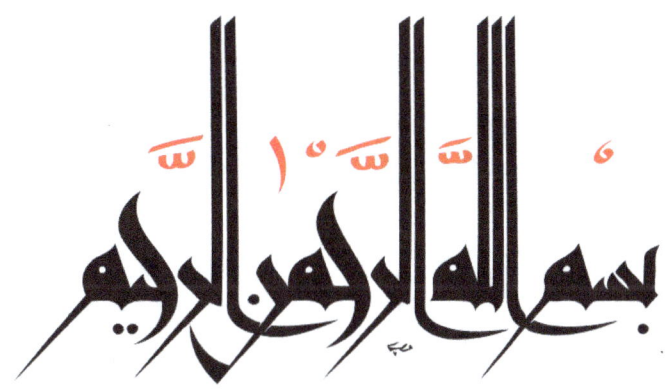

In the name of God, the Most Gracious, the Most Merciful

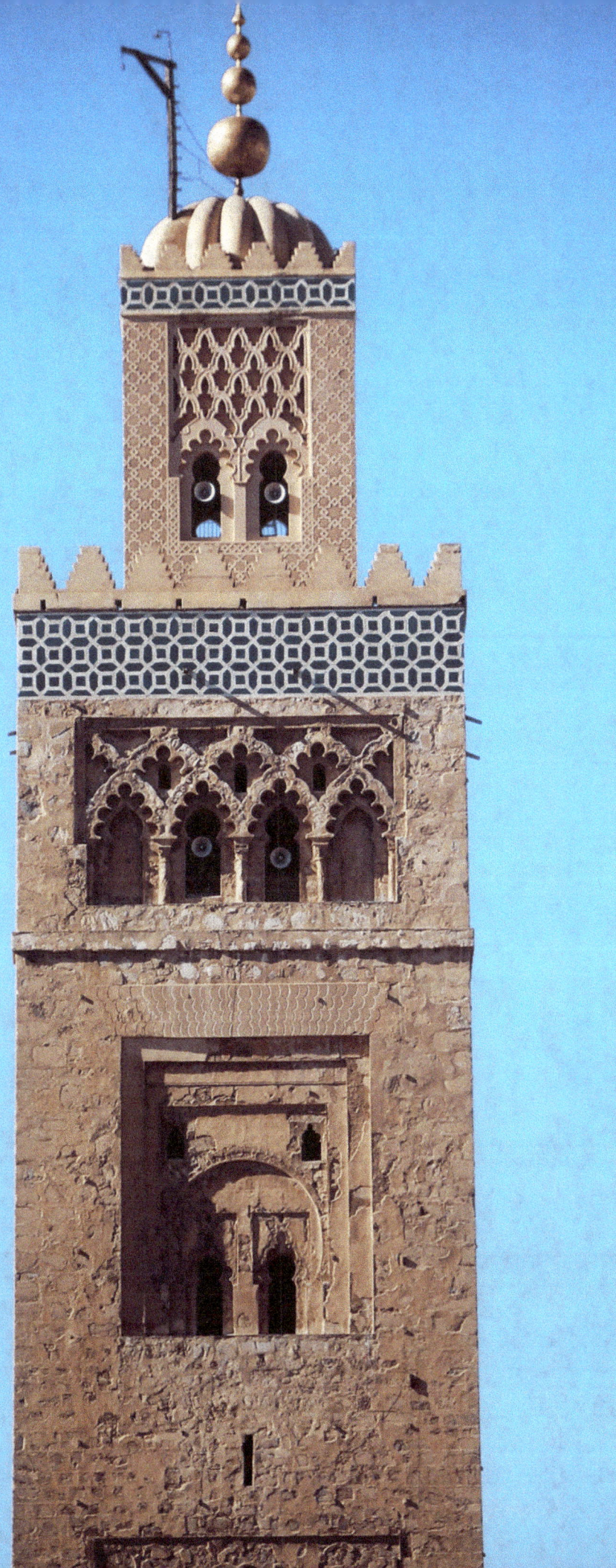

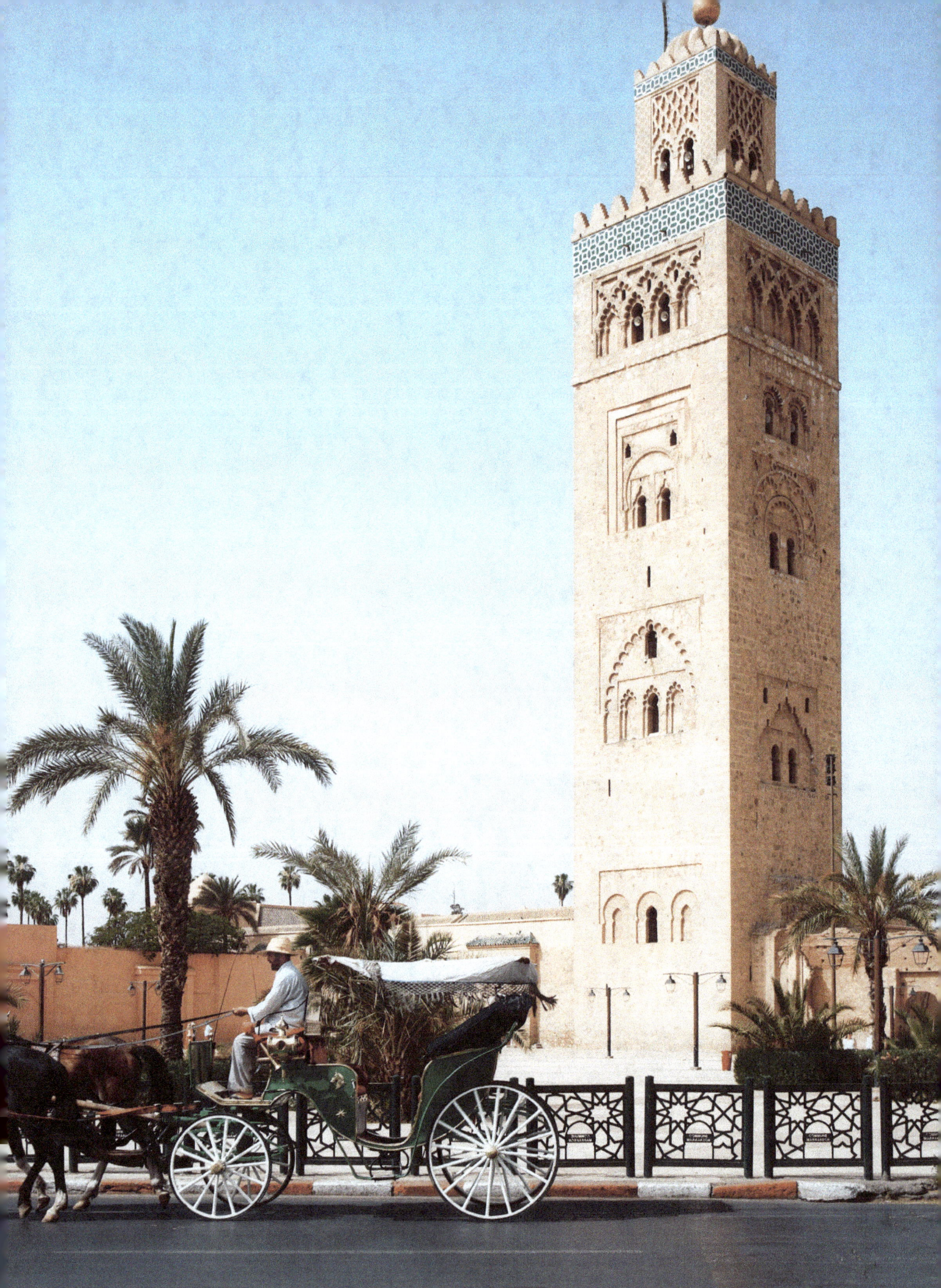

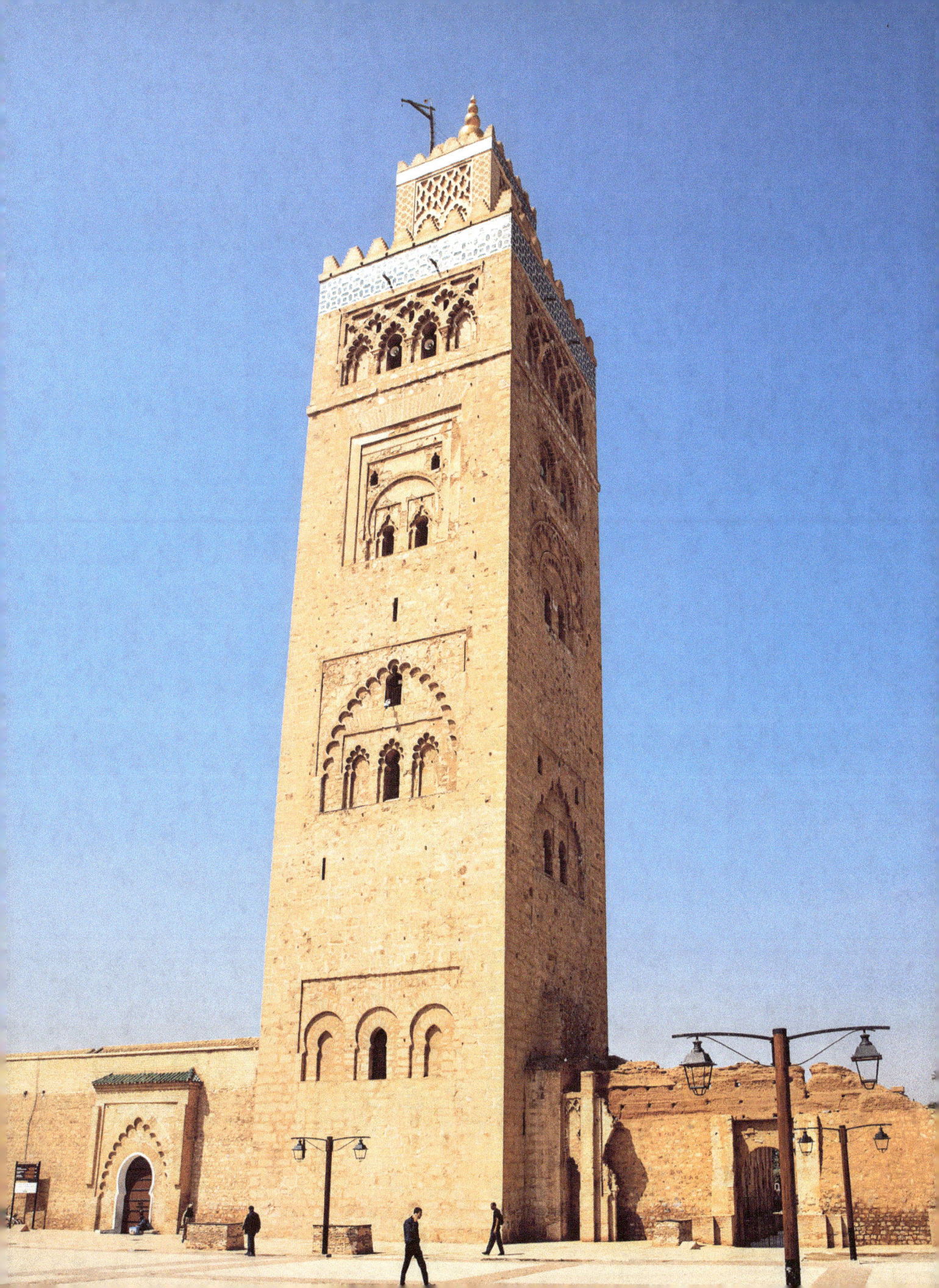

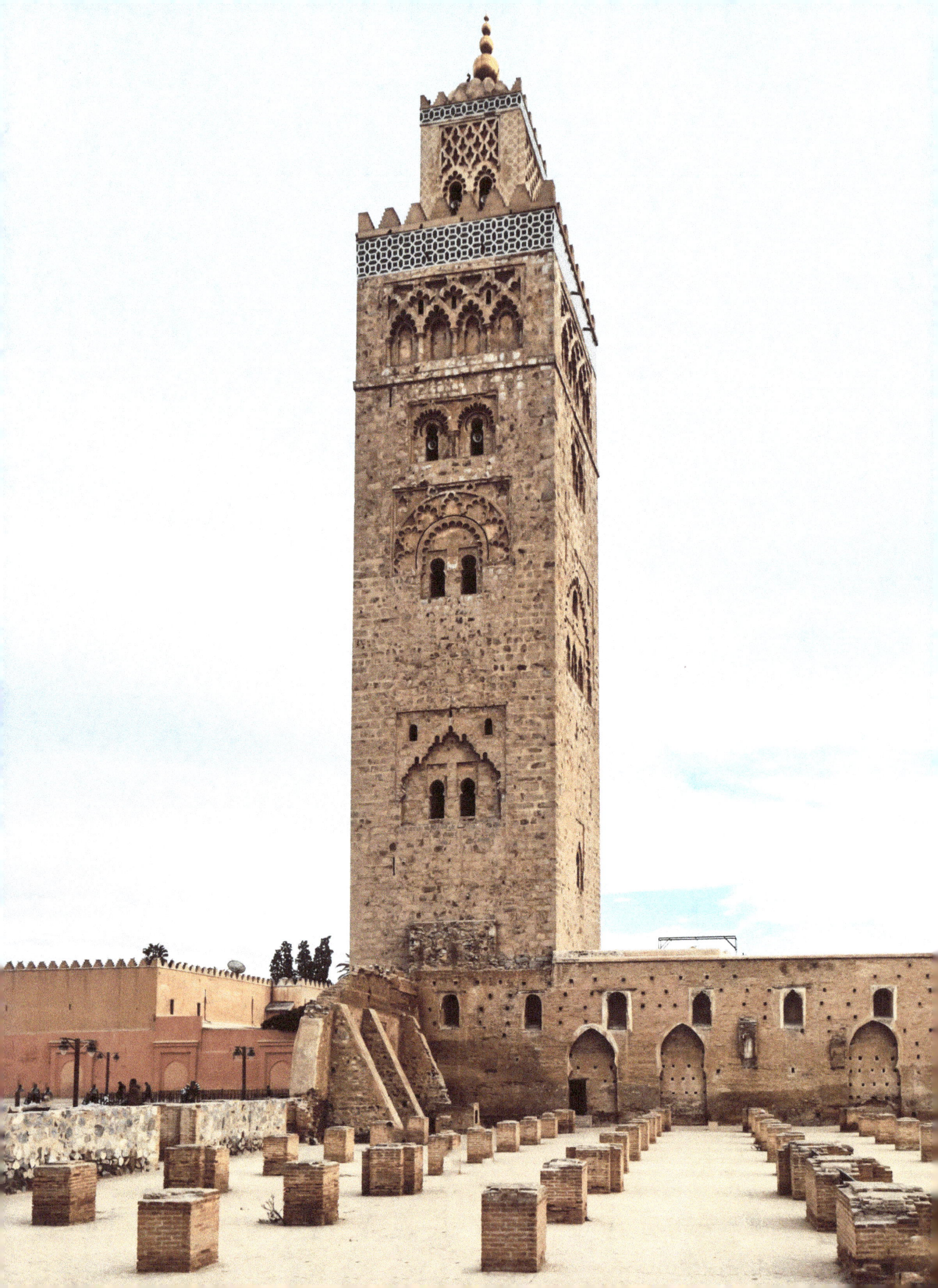

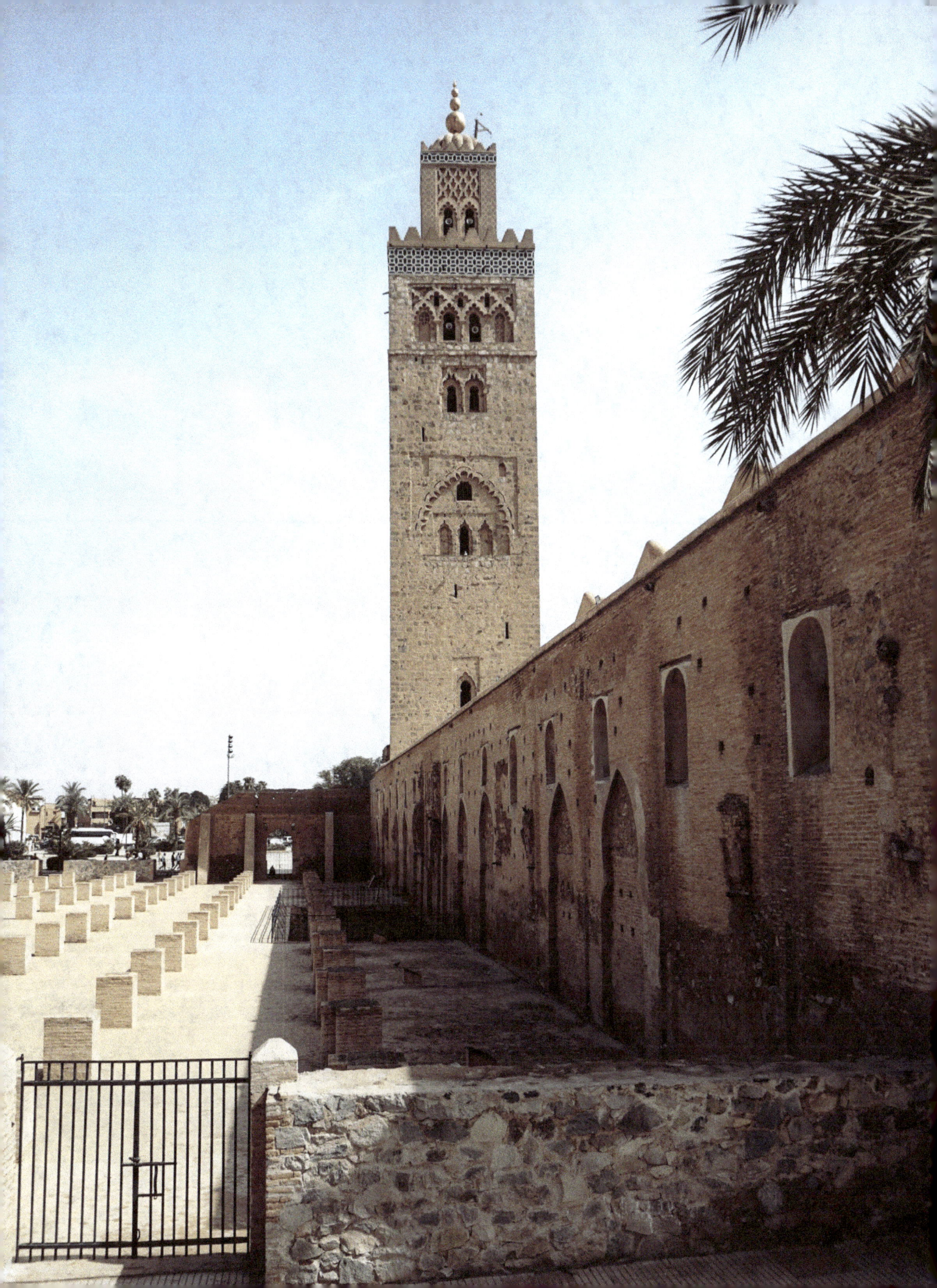

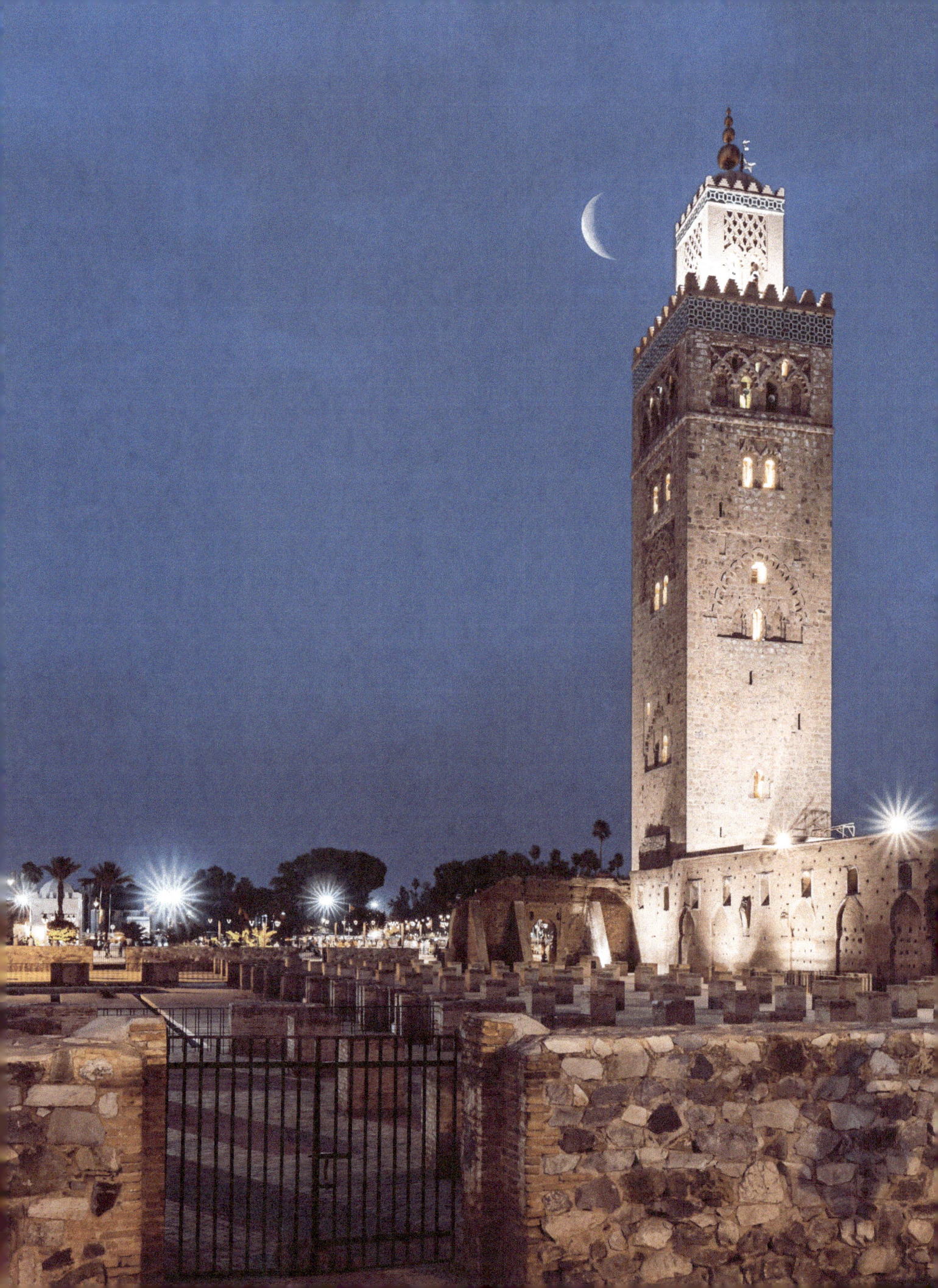

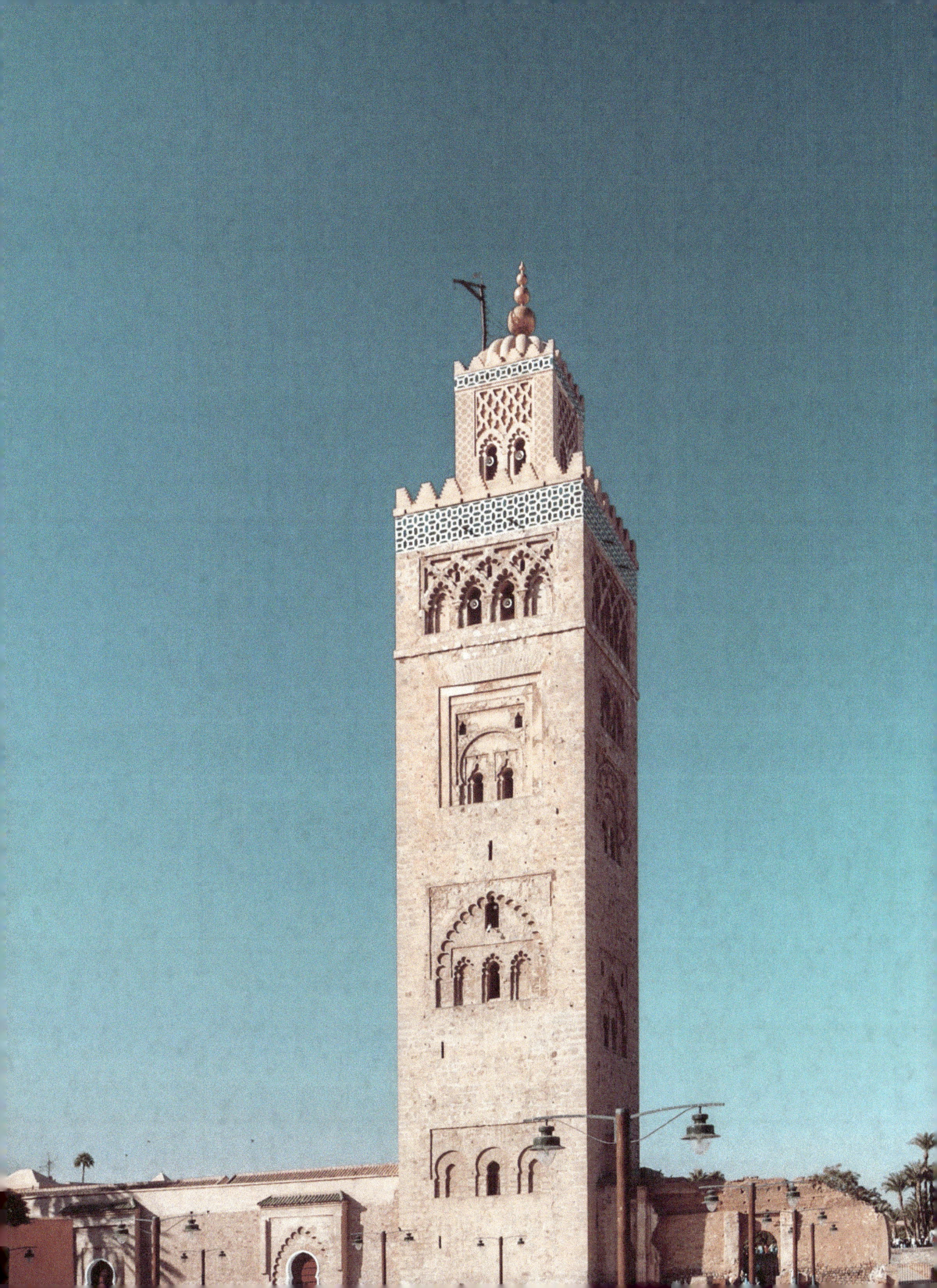

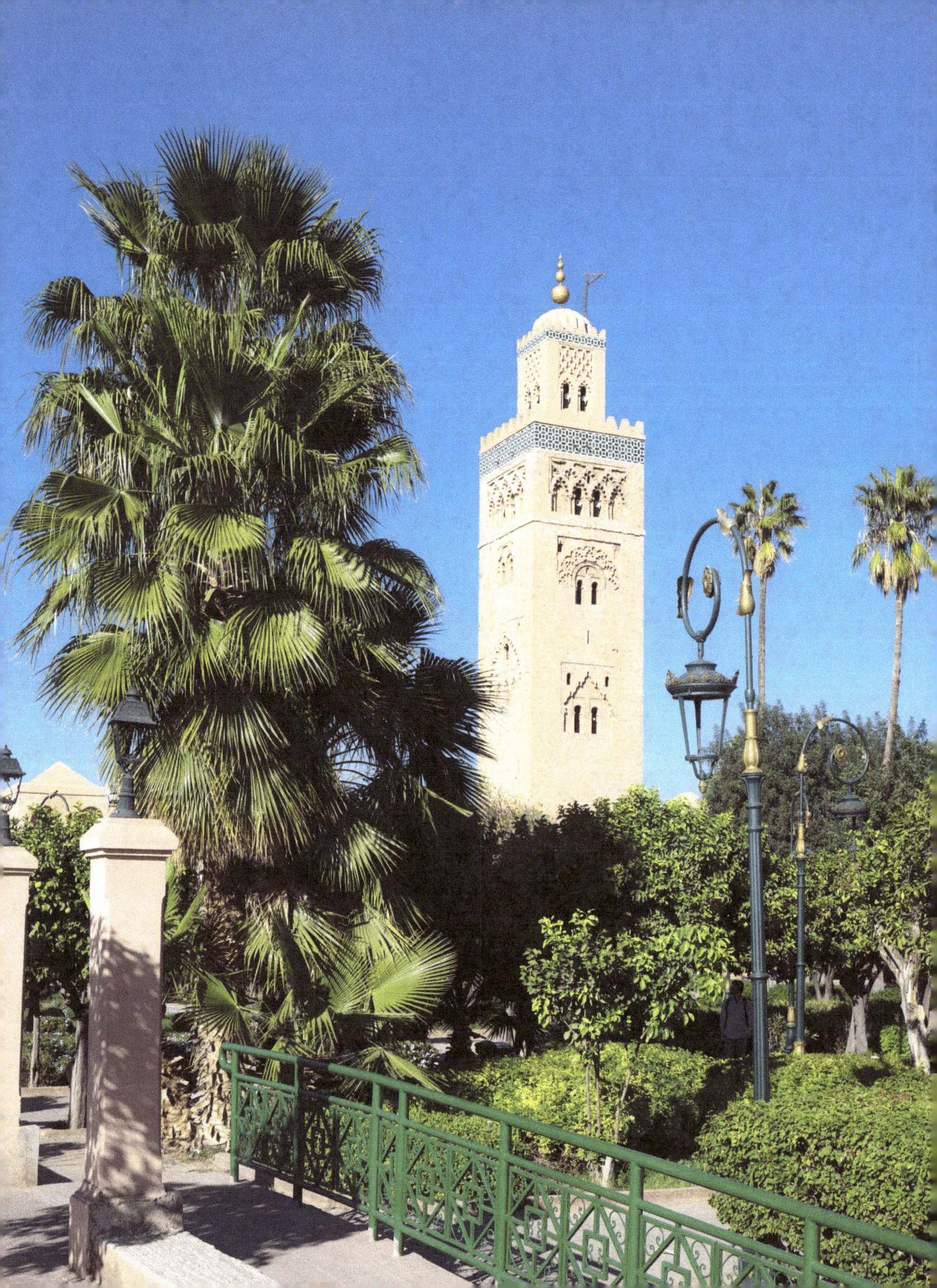

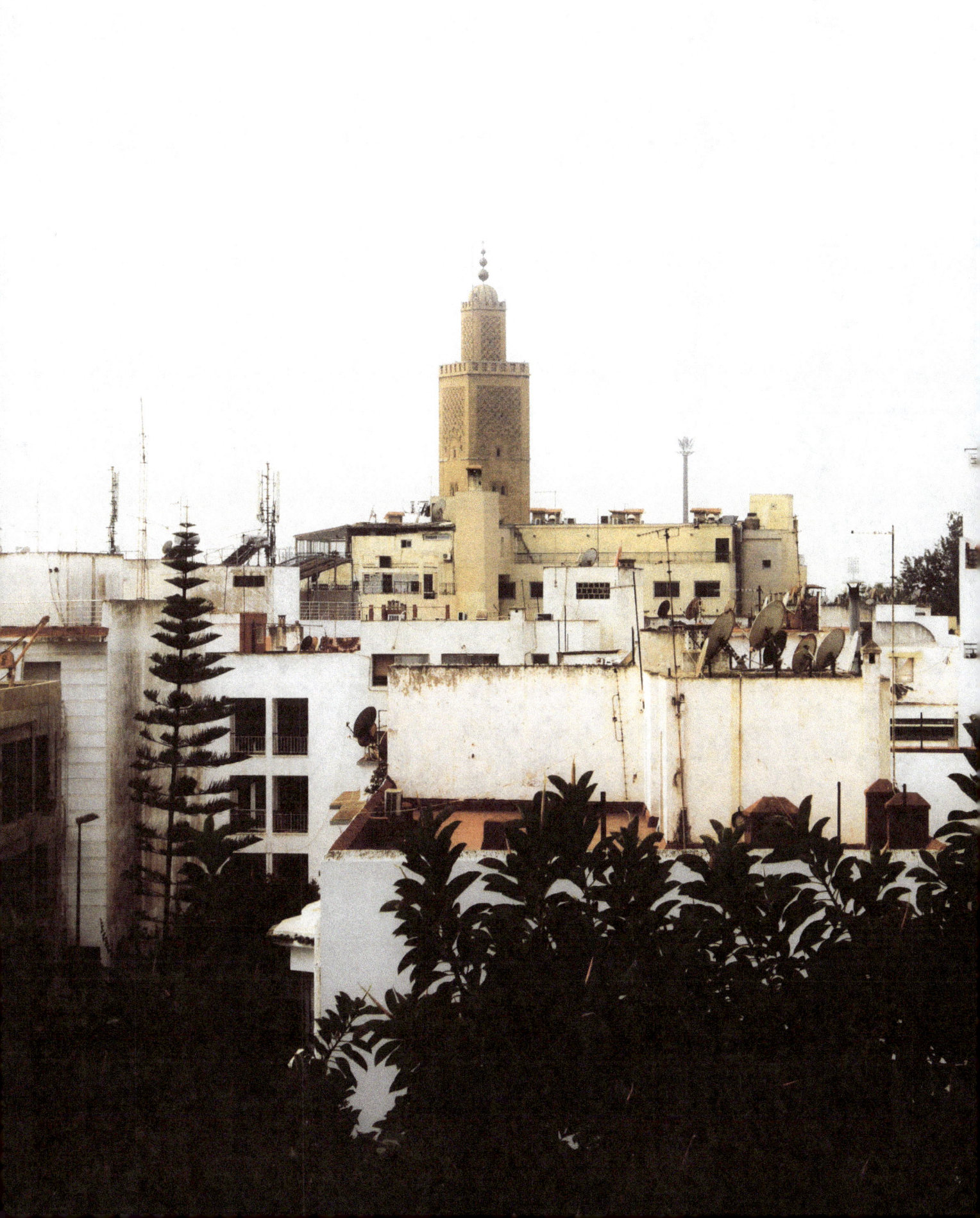

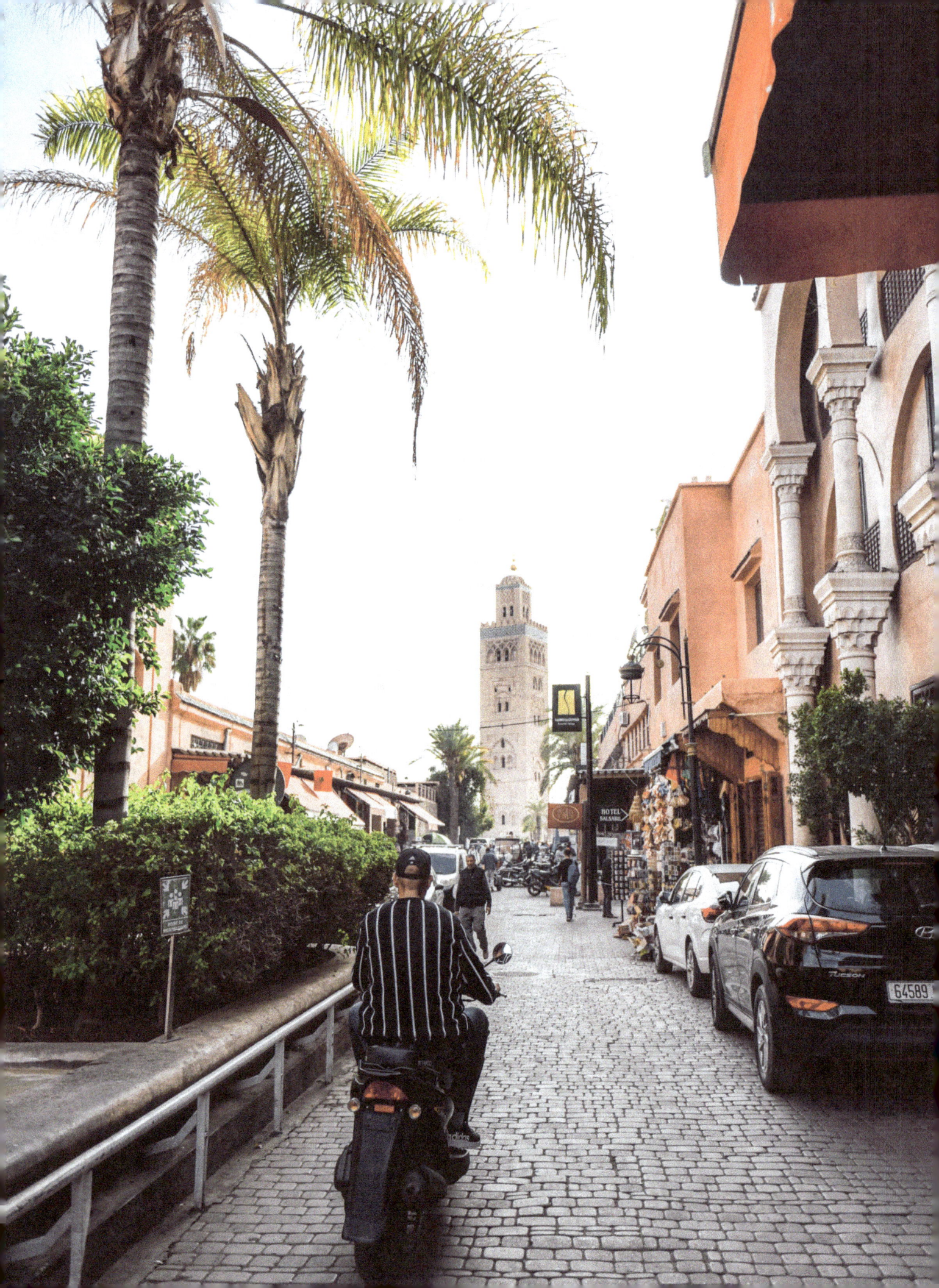

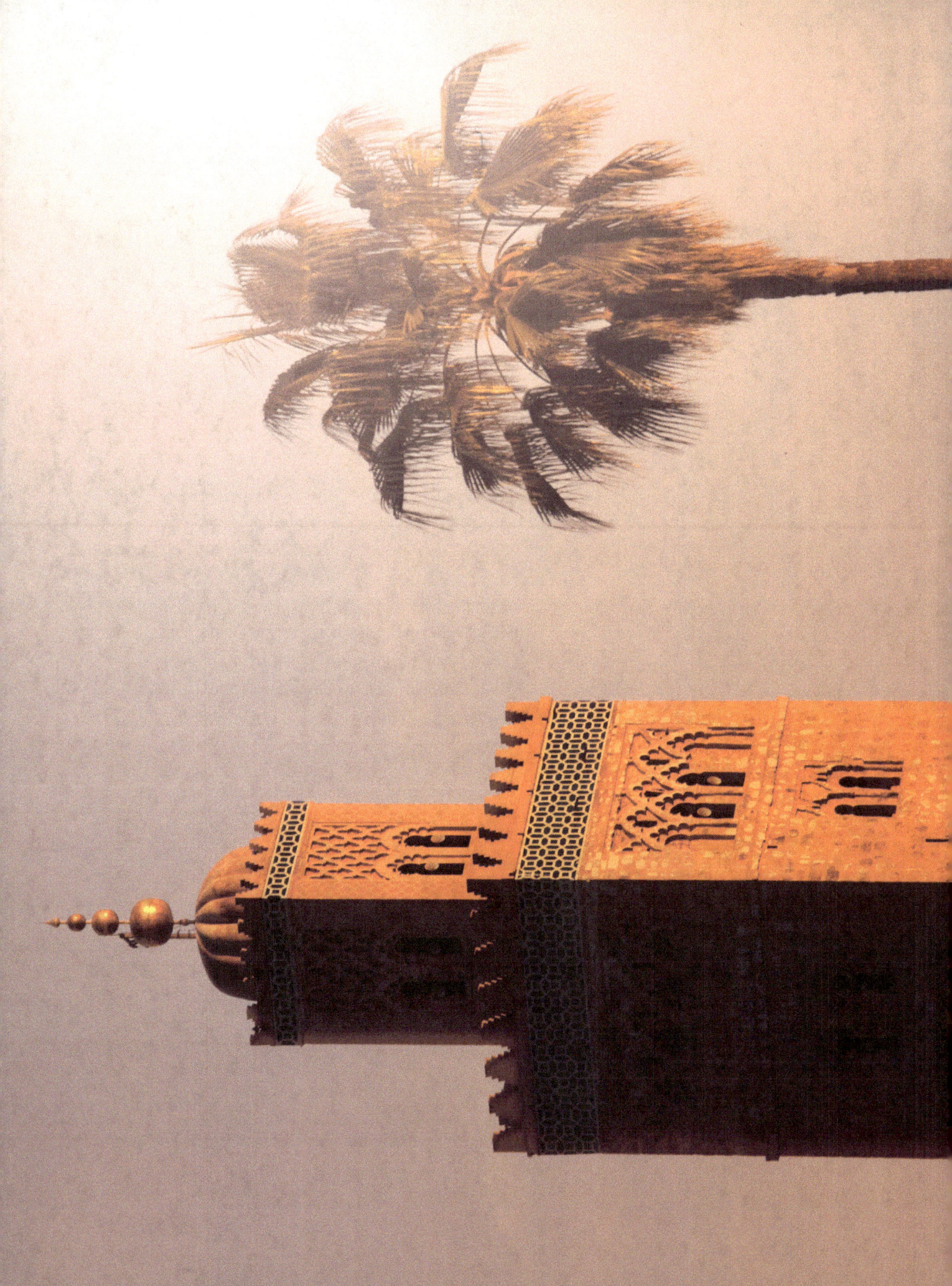

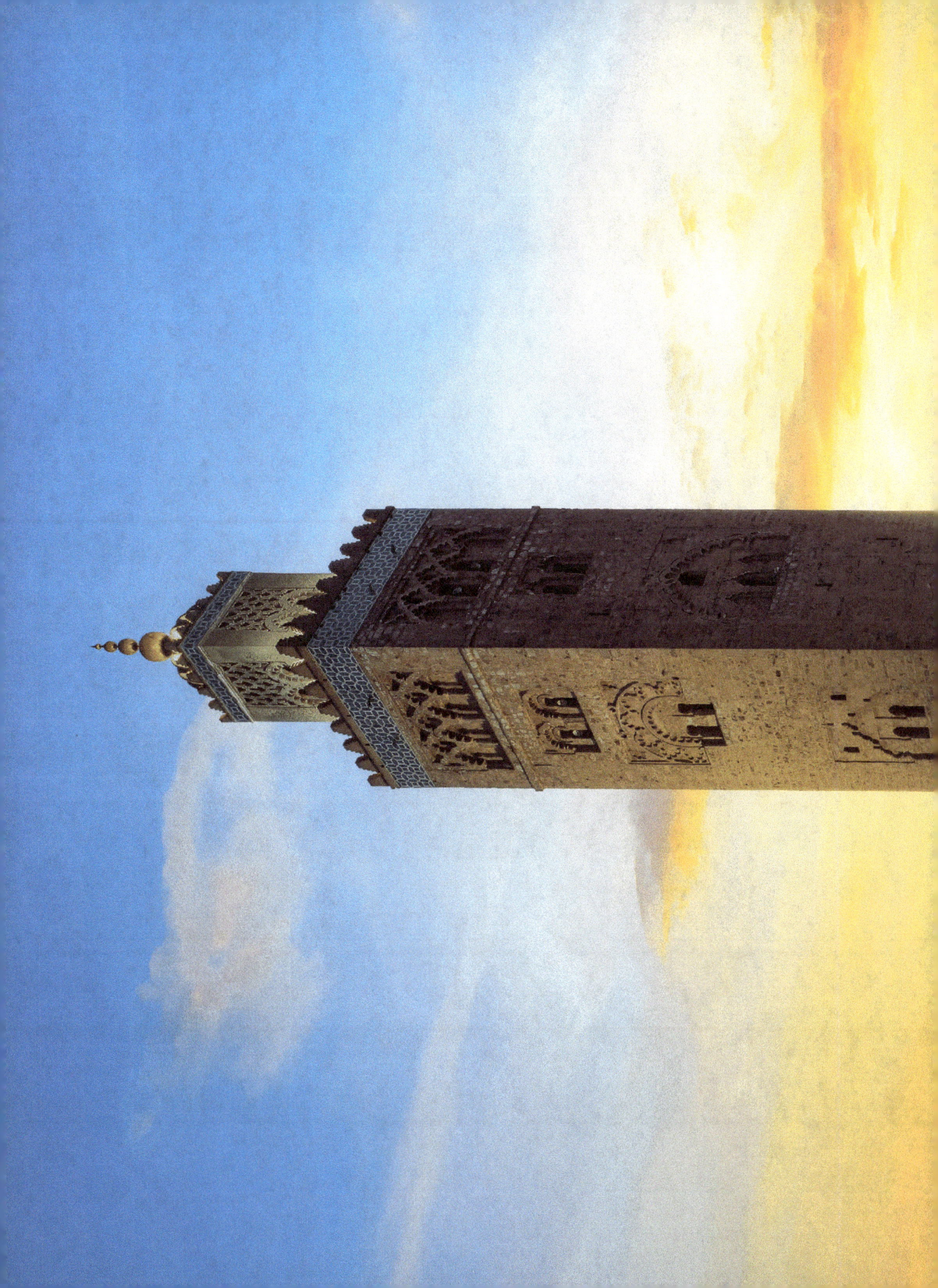

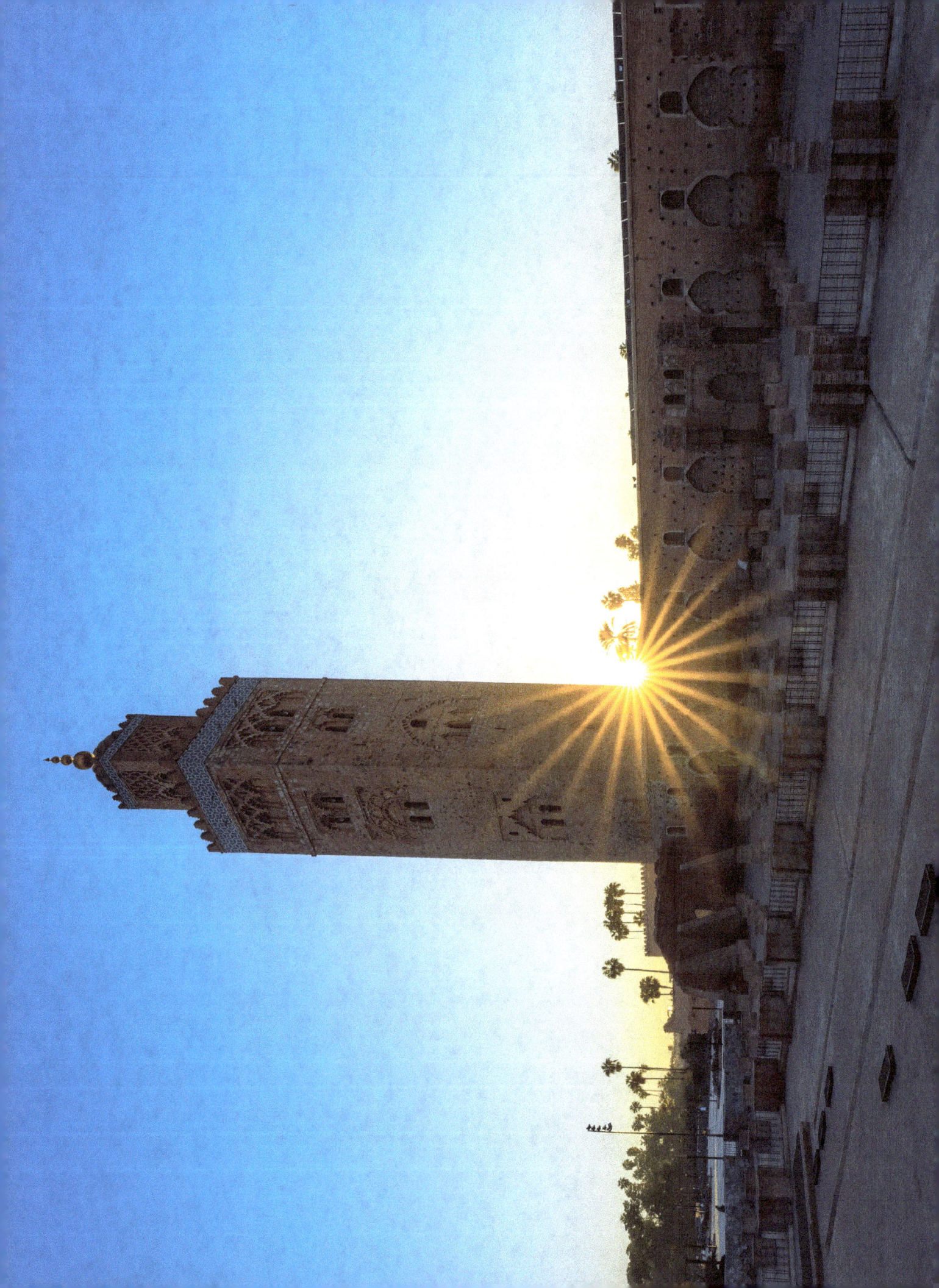

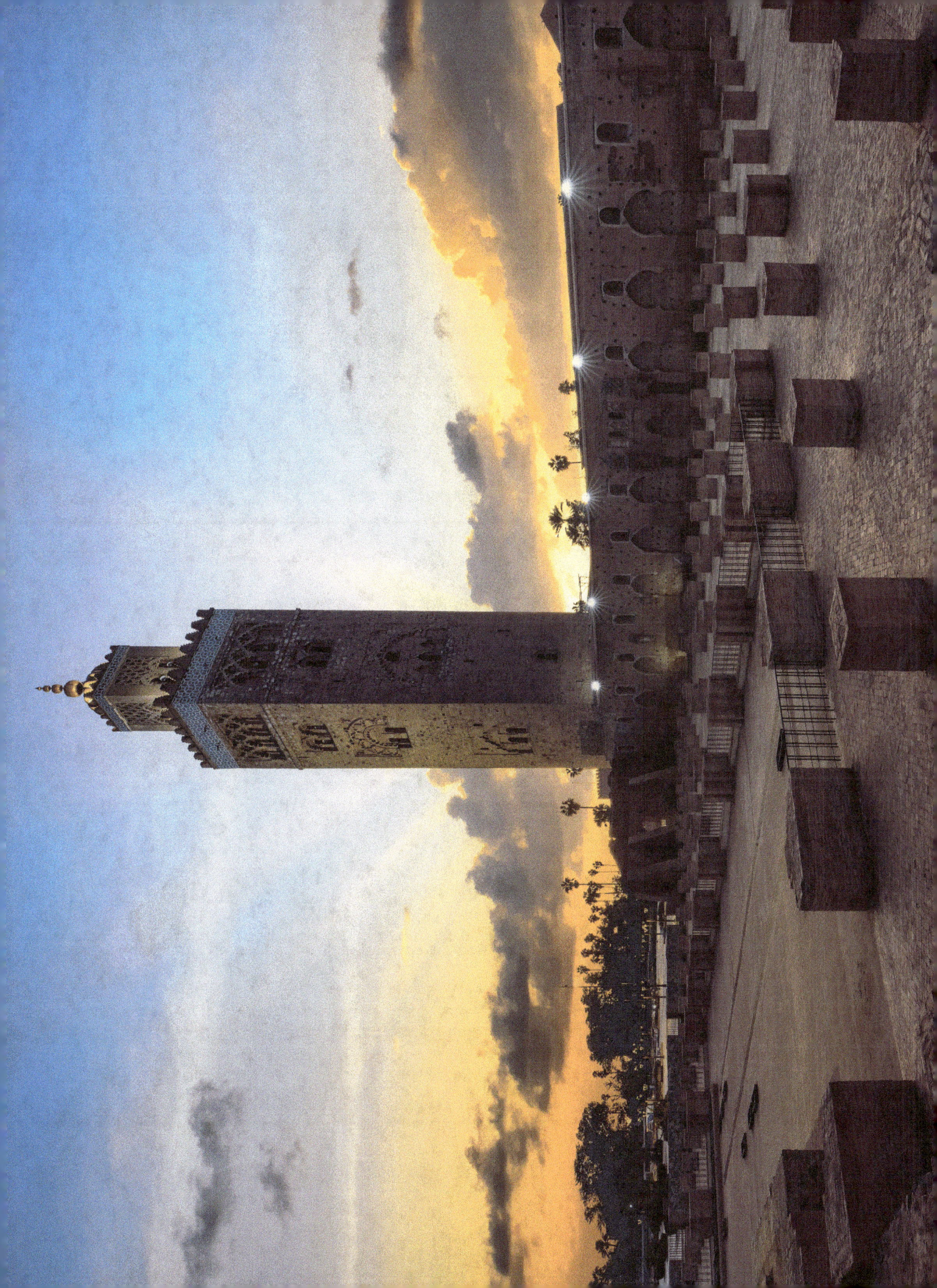

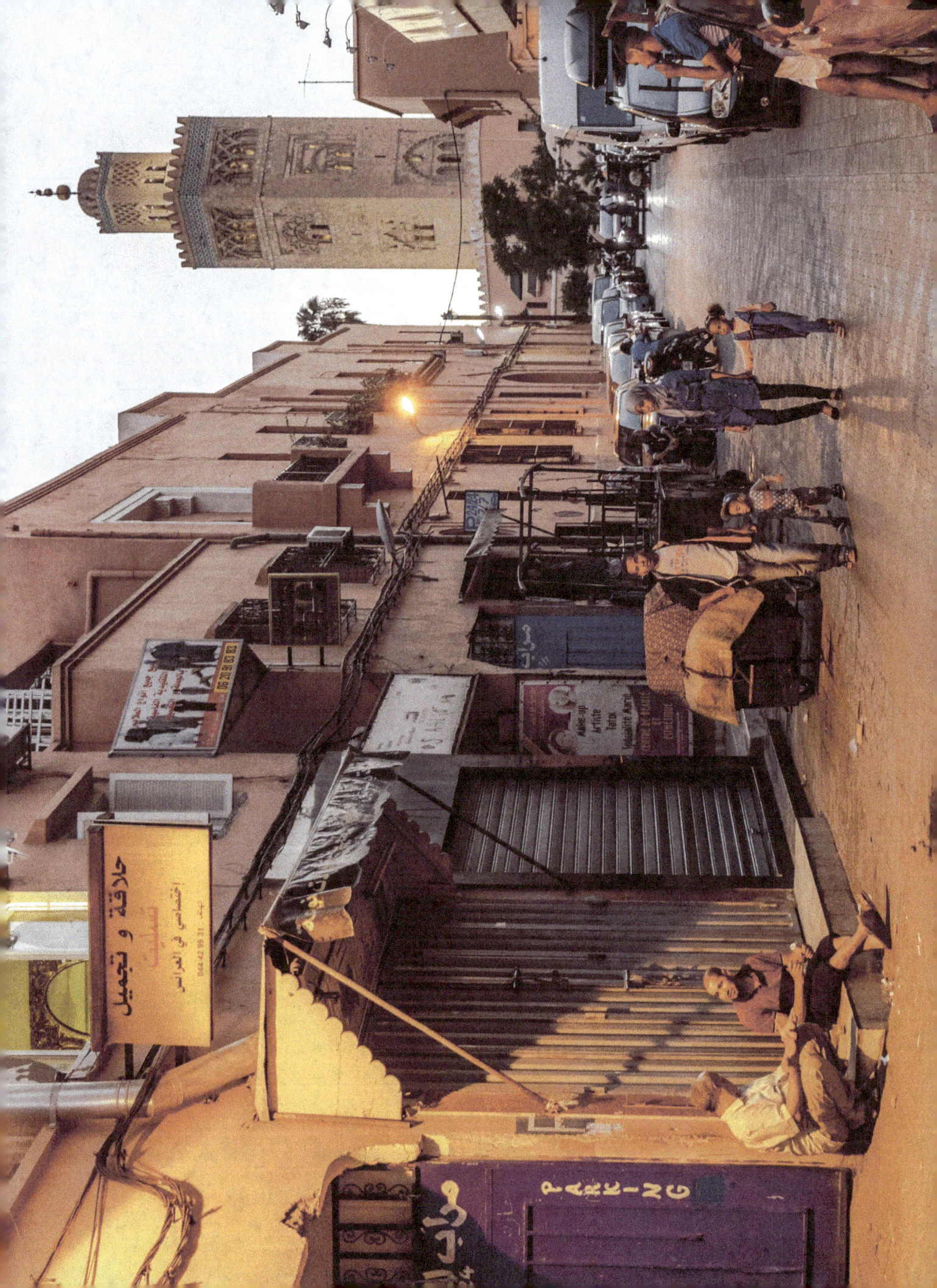

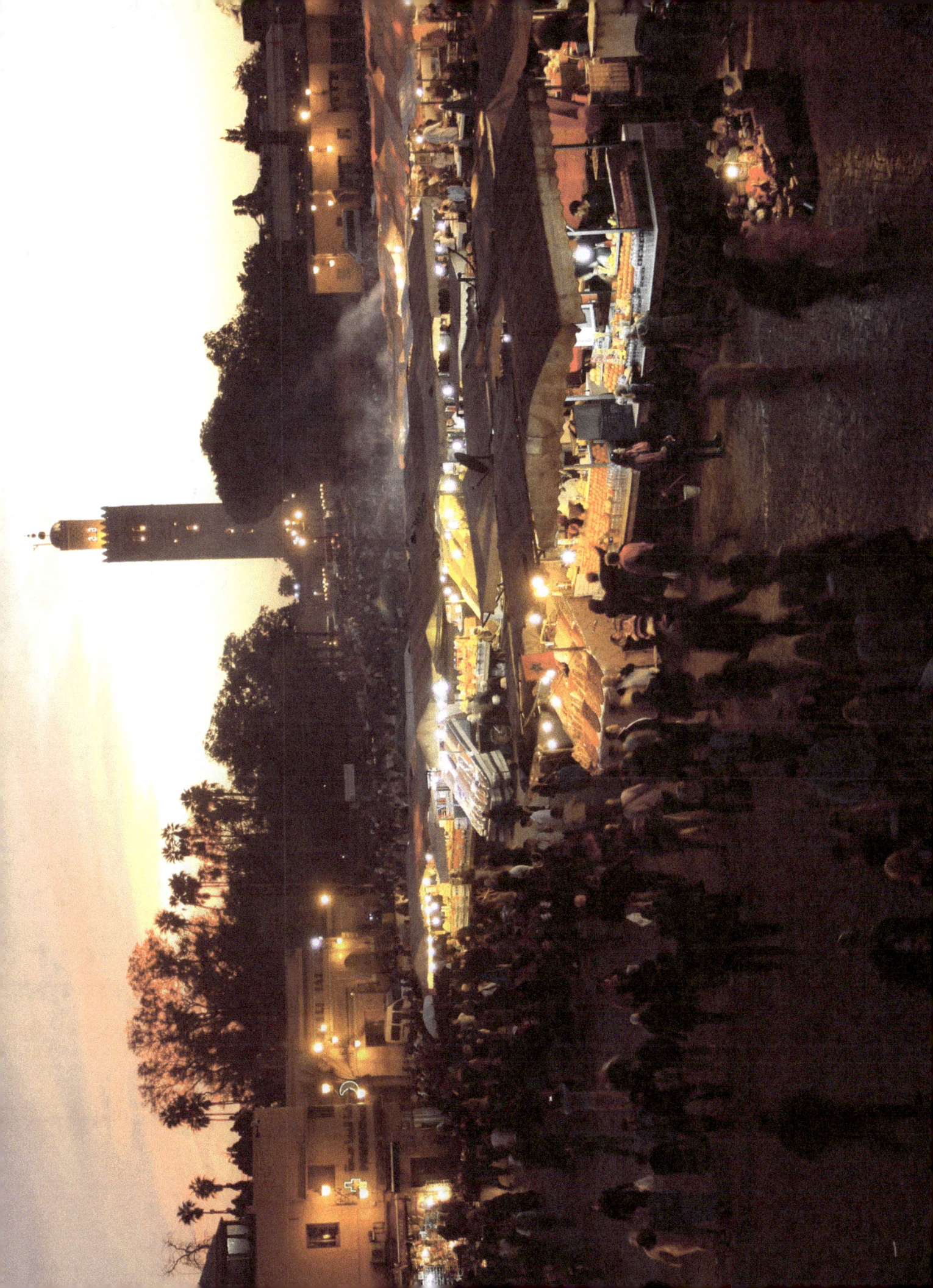

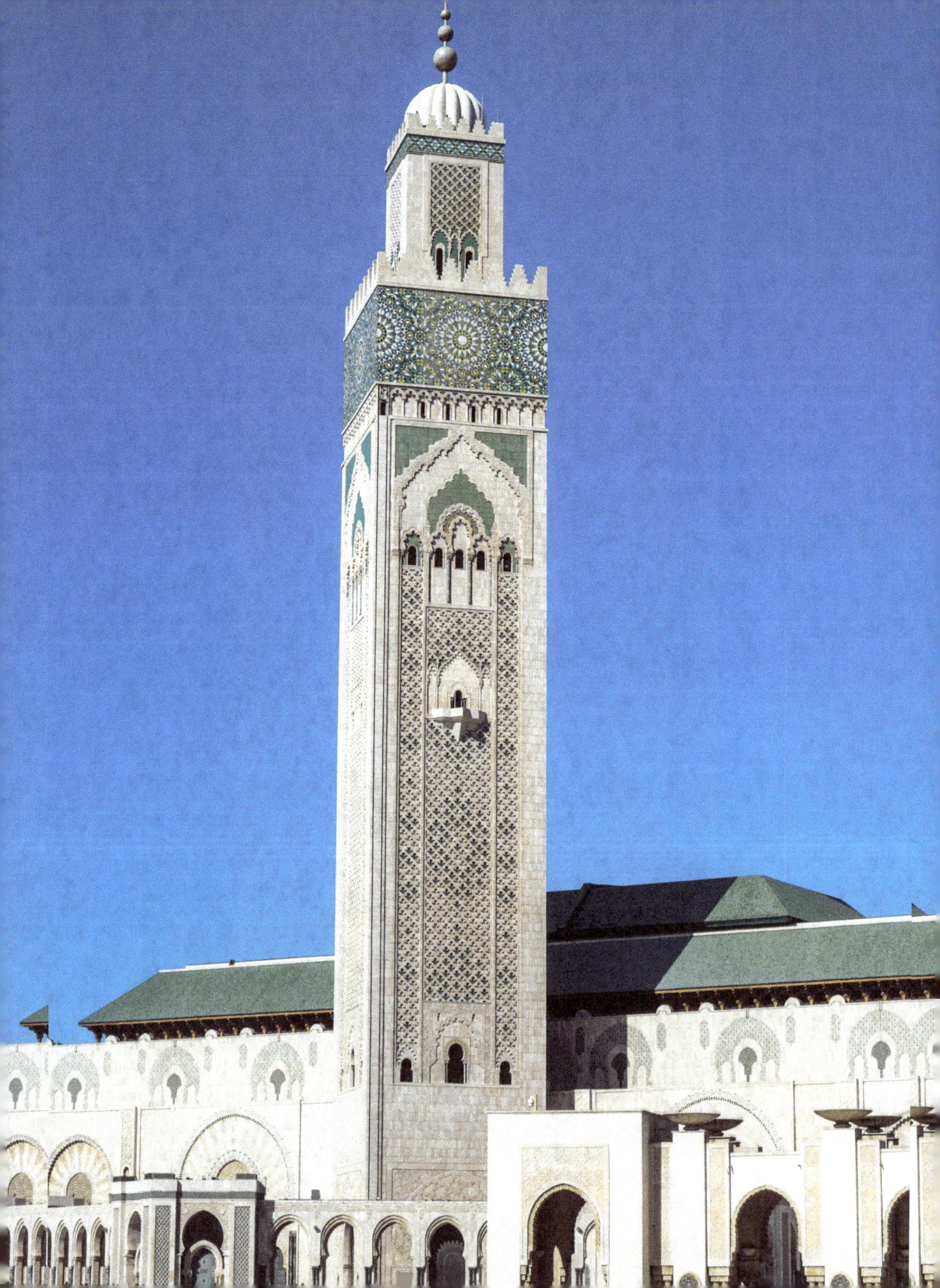

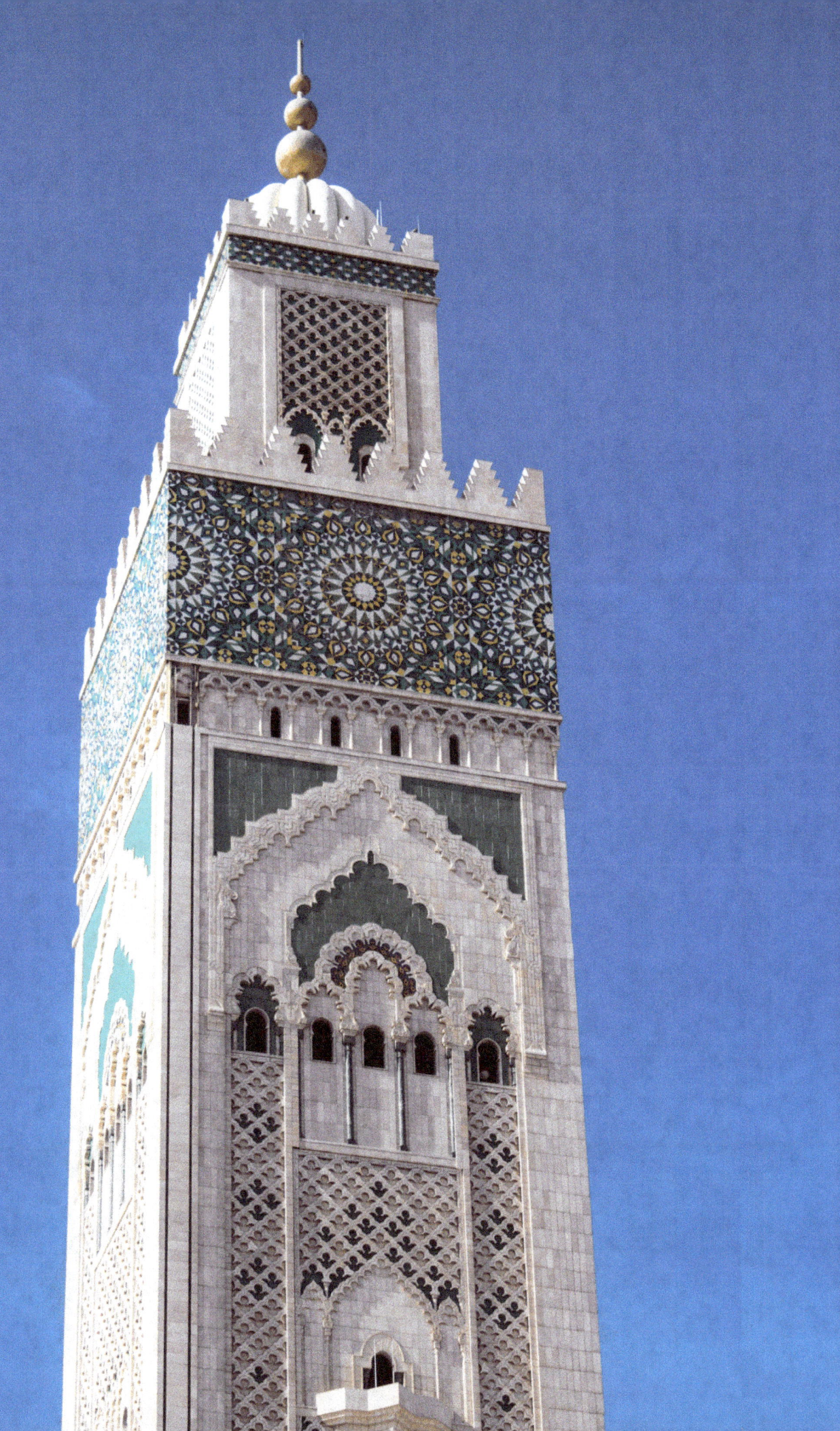

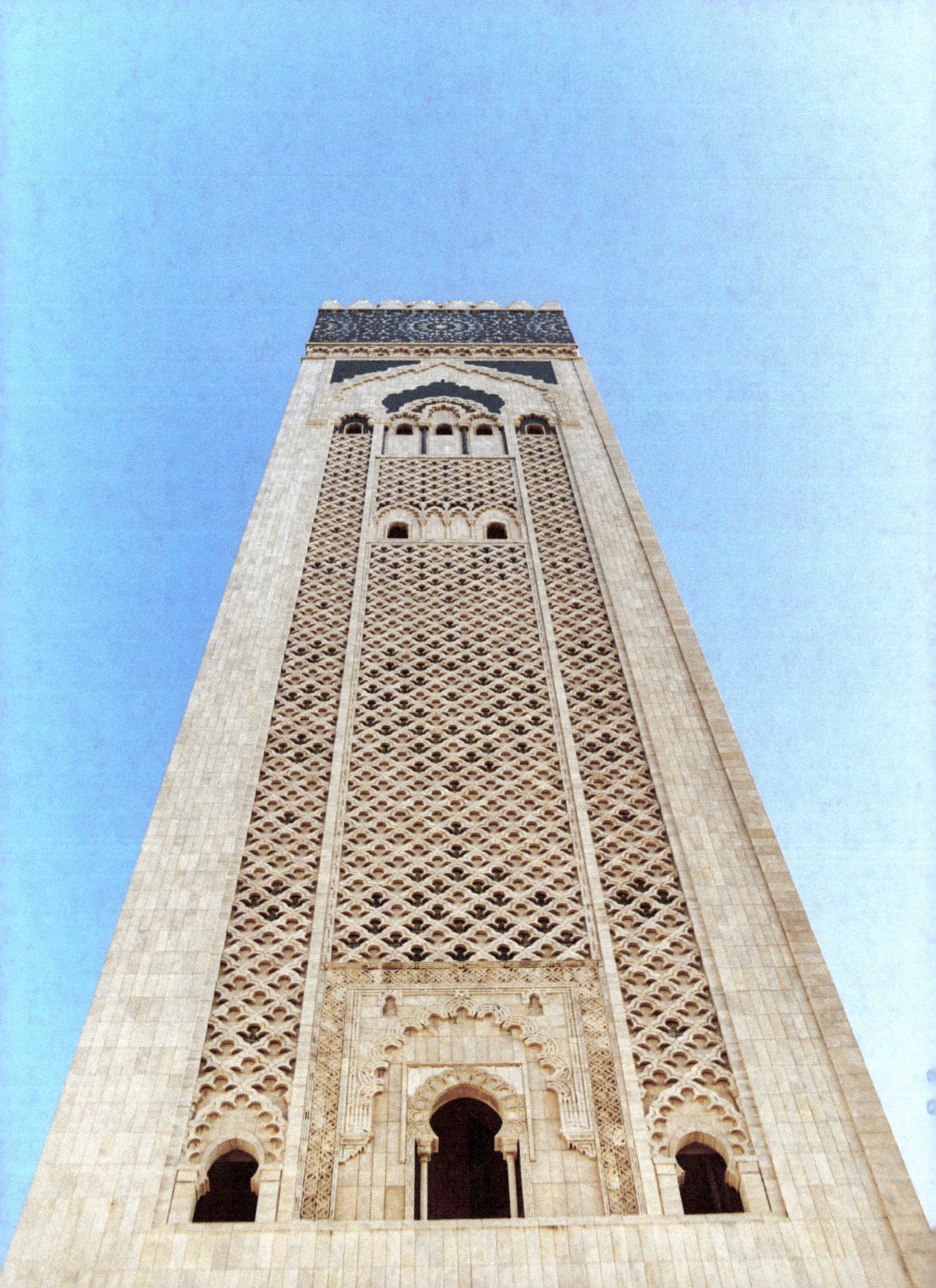

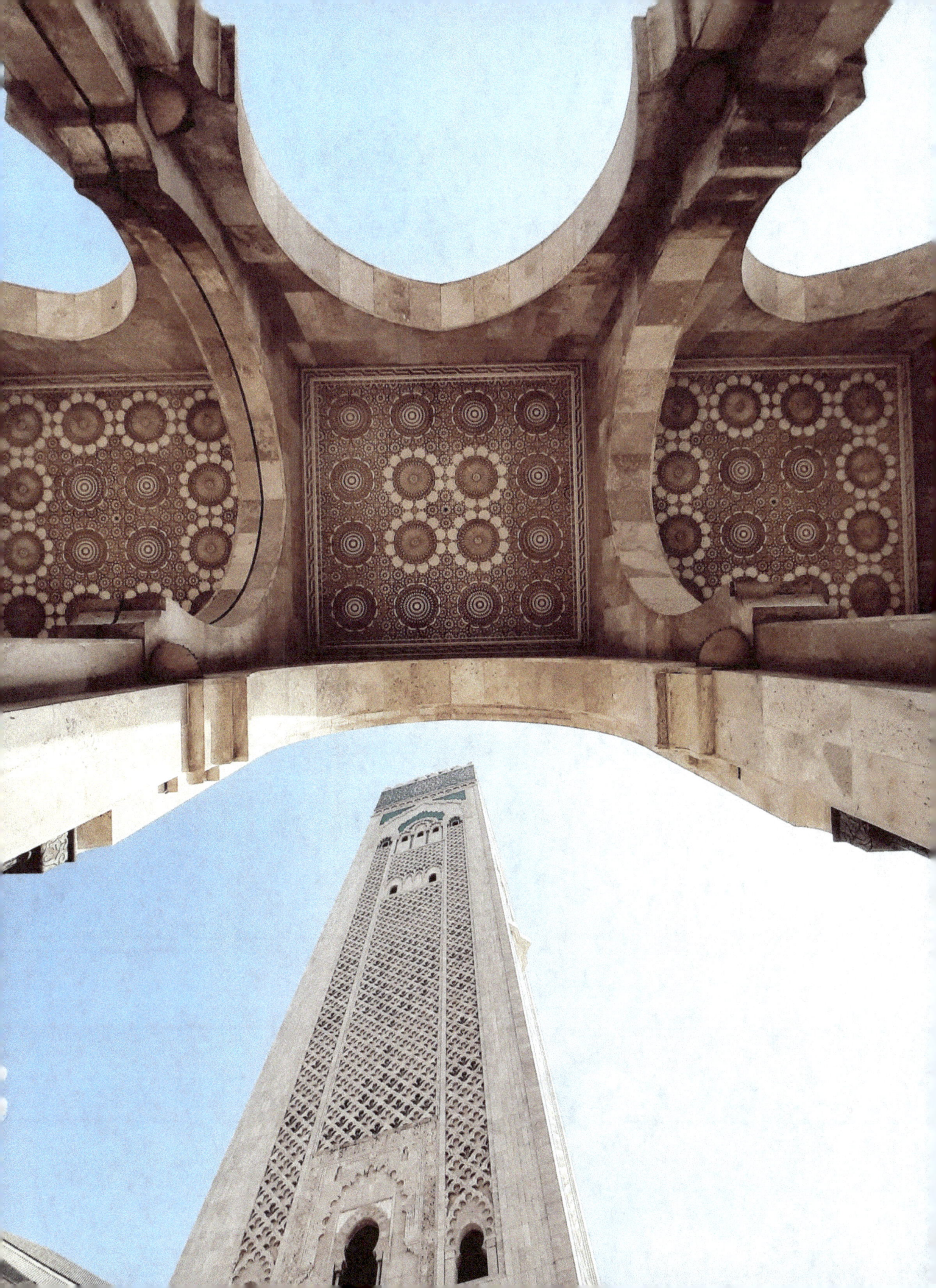

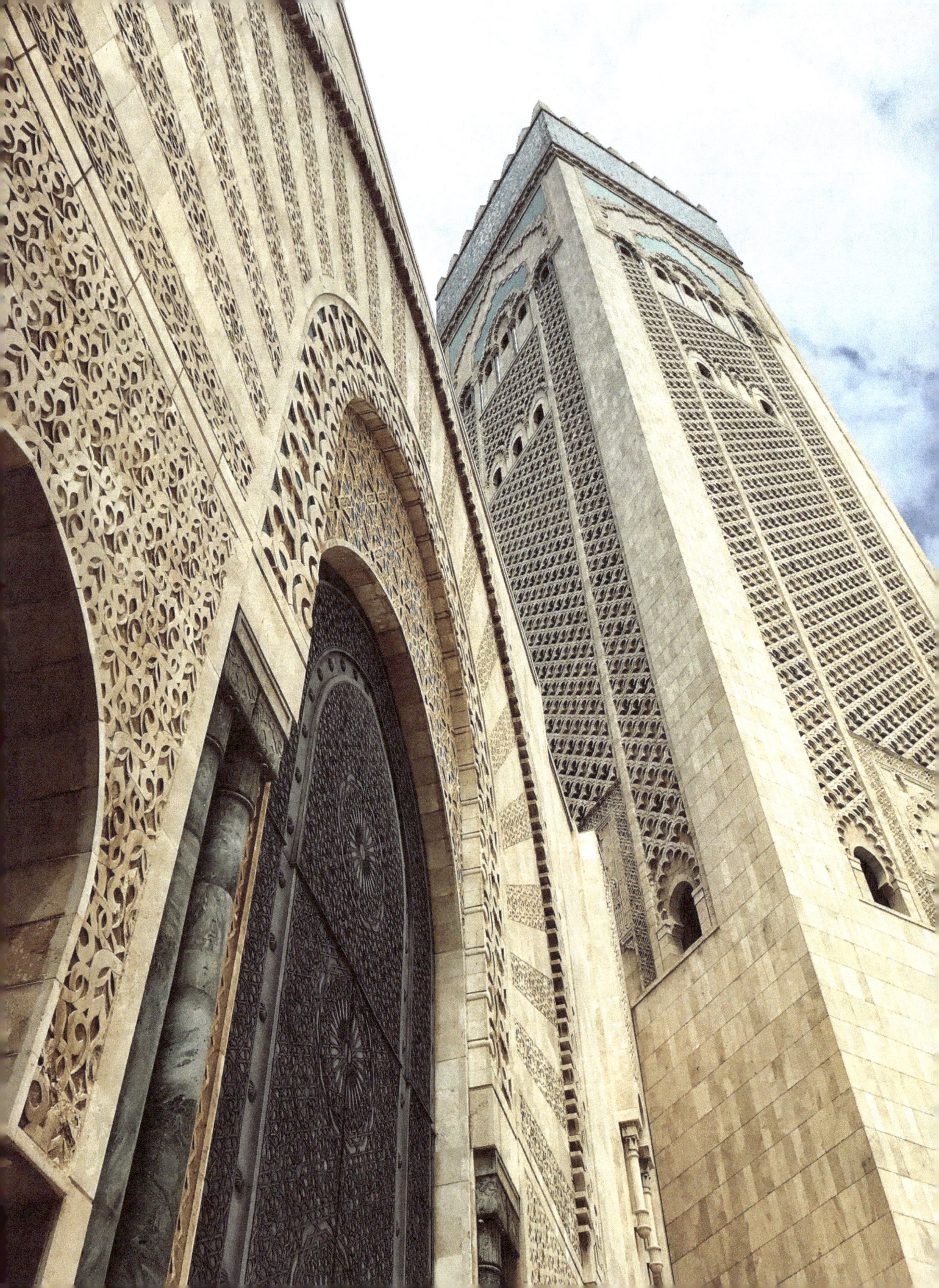

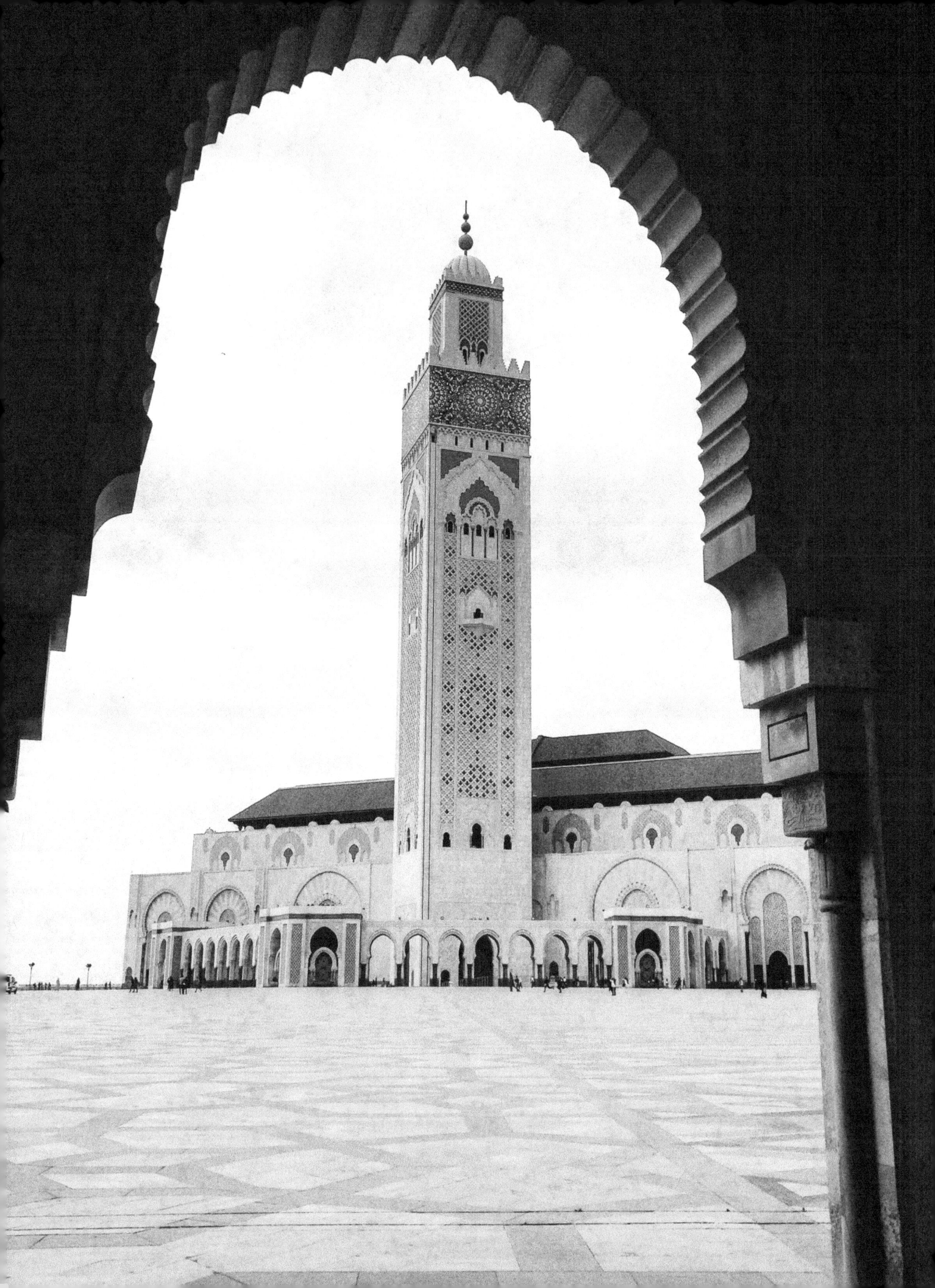

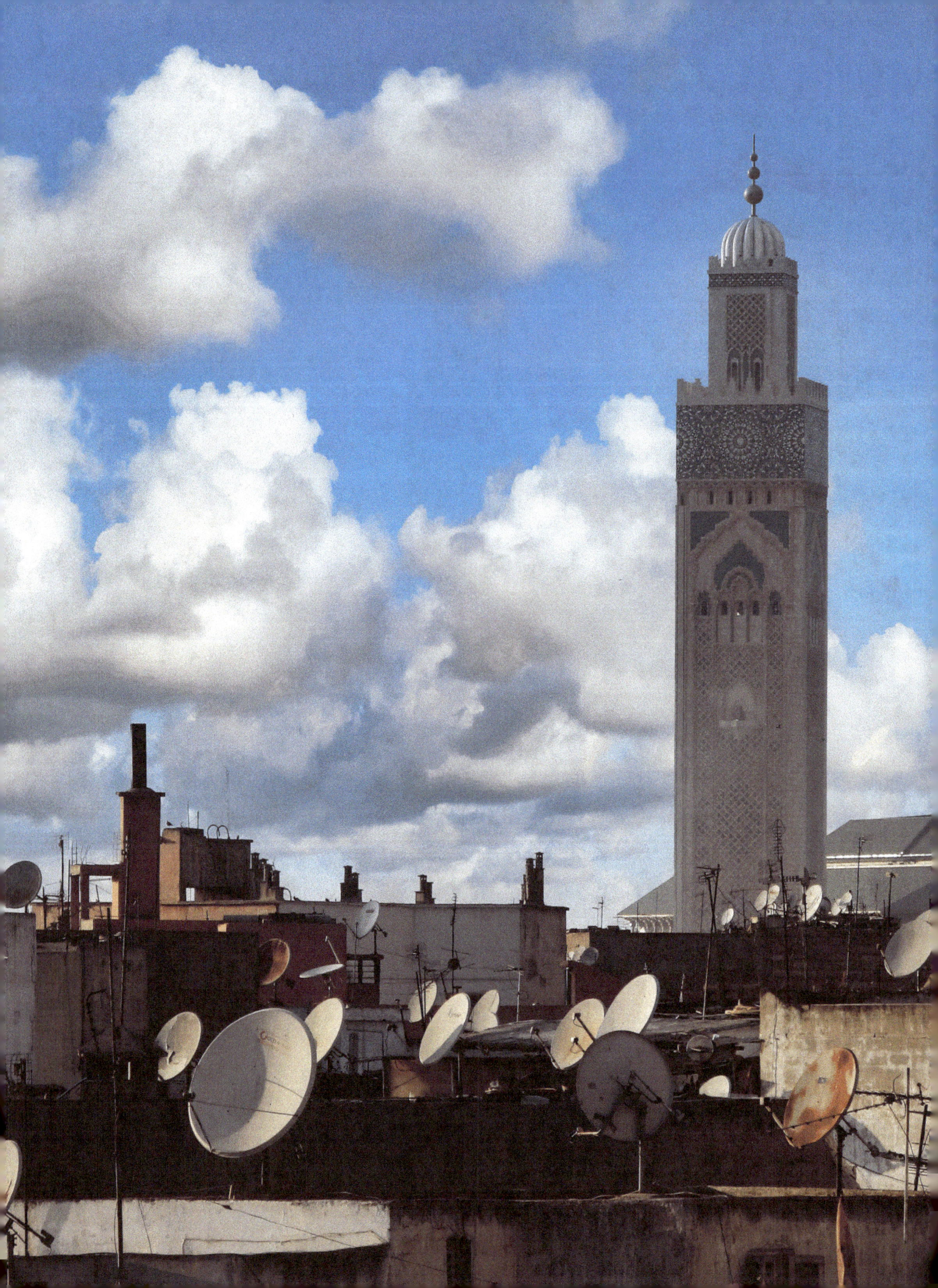

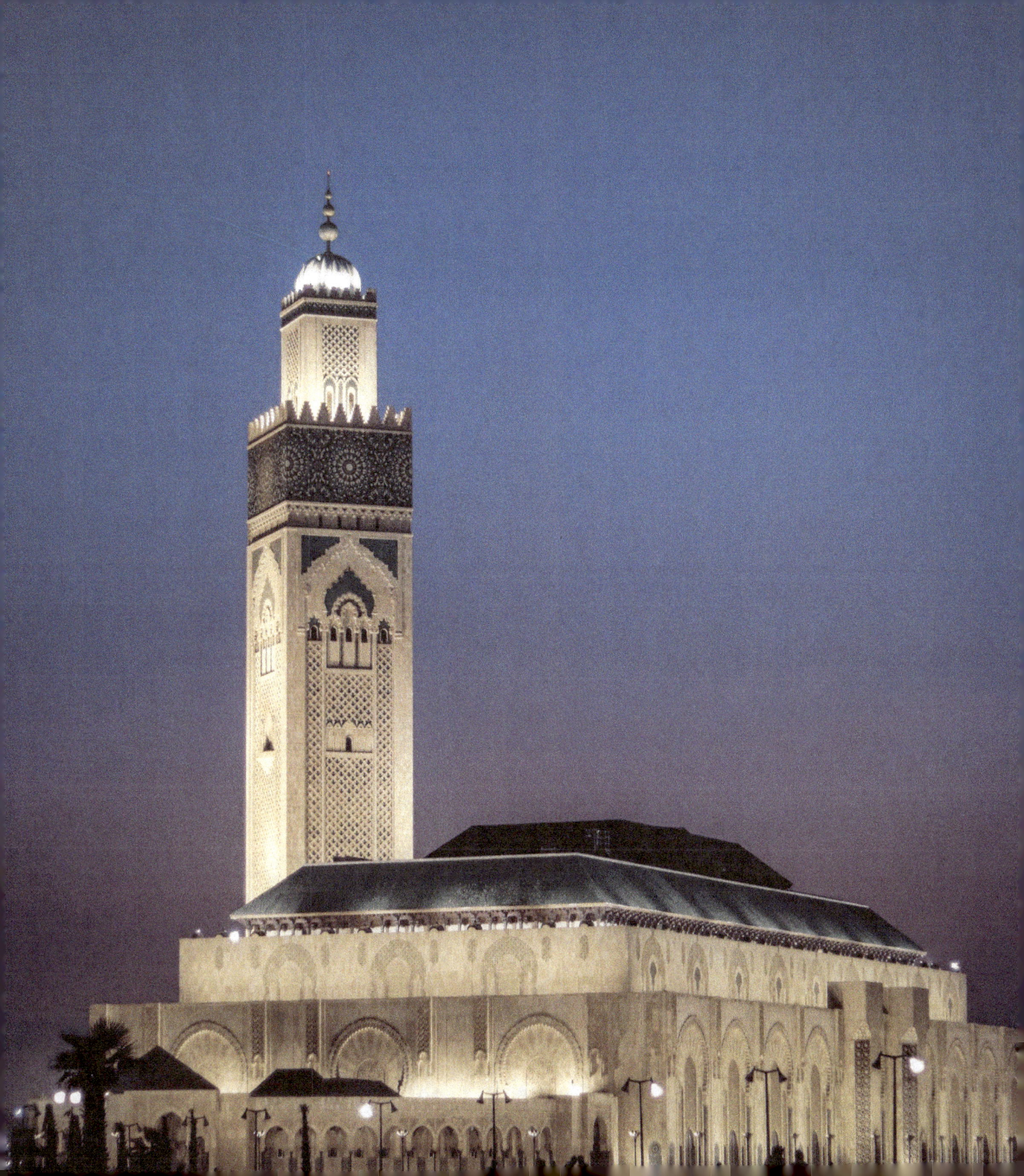

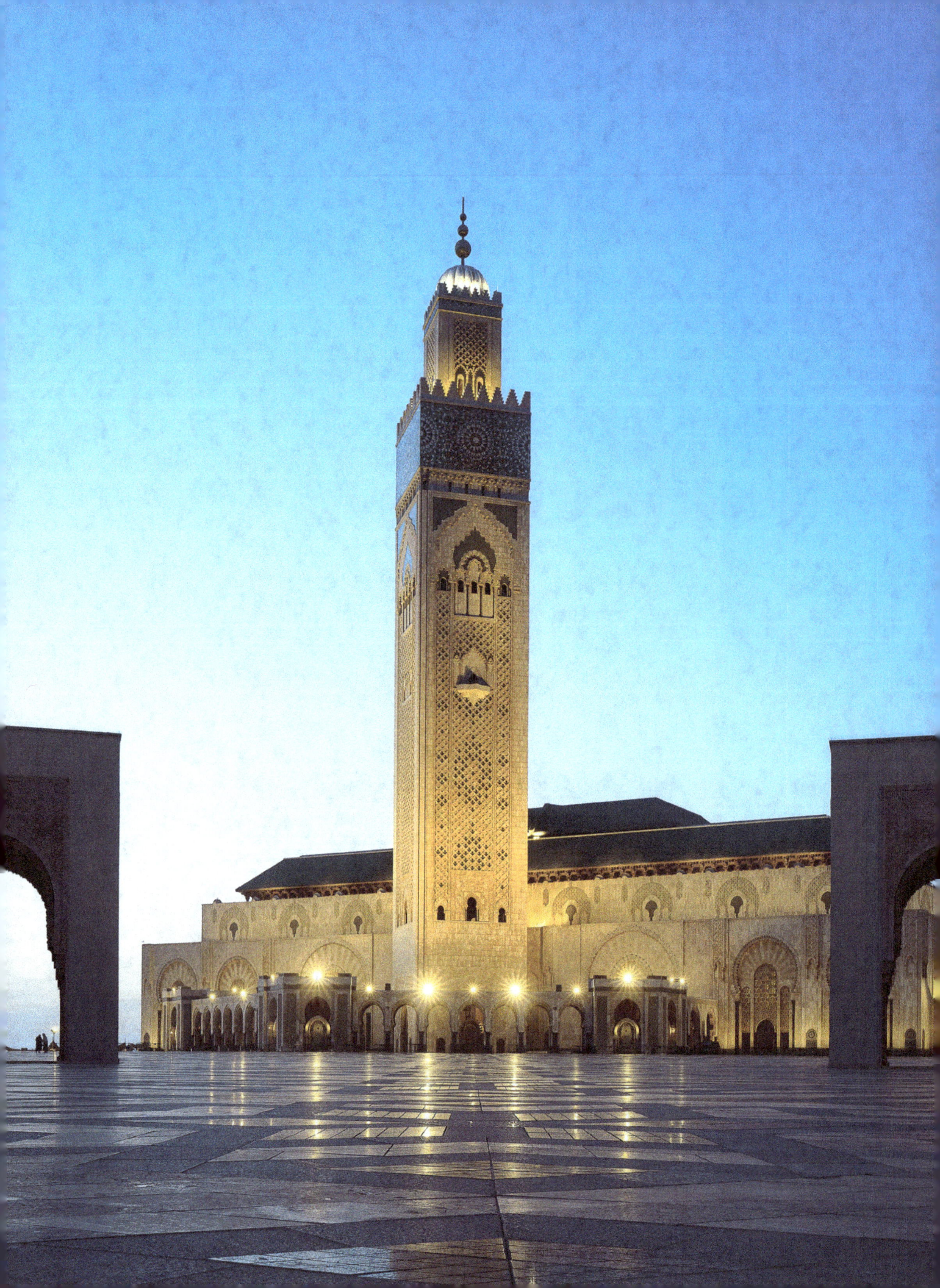

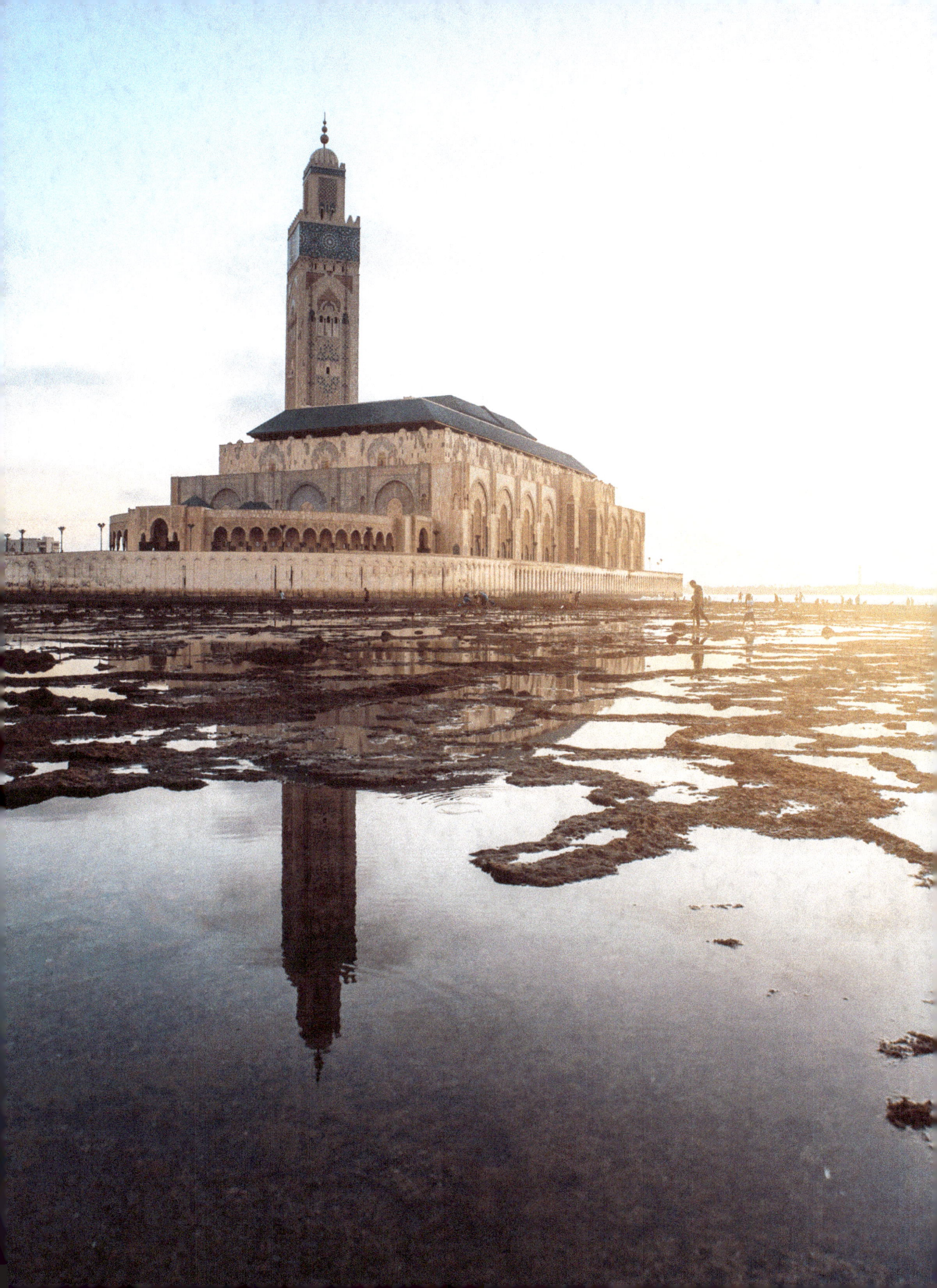

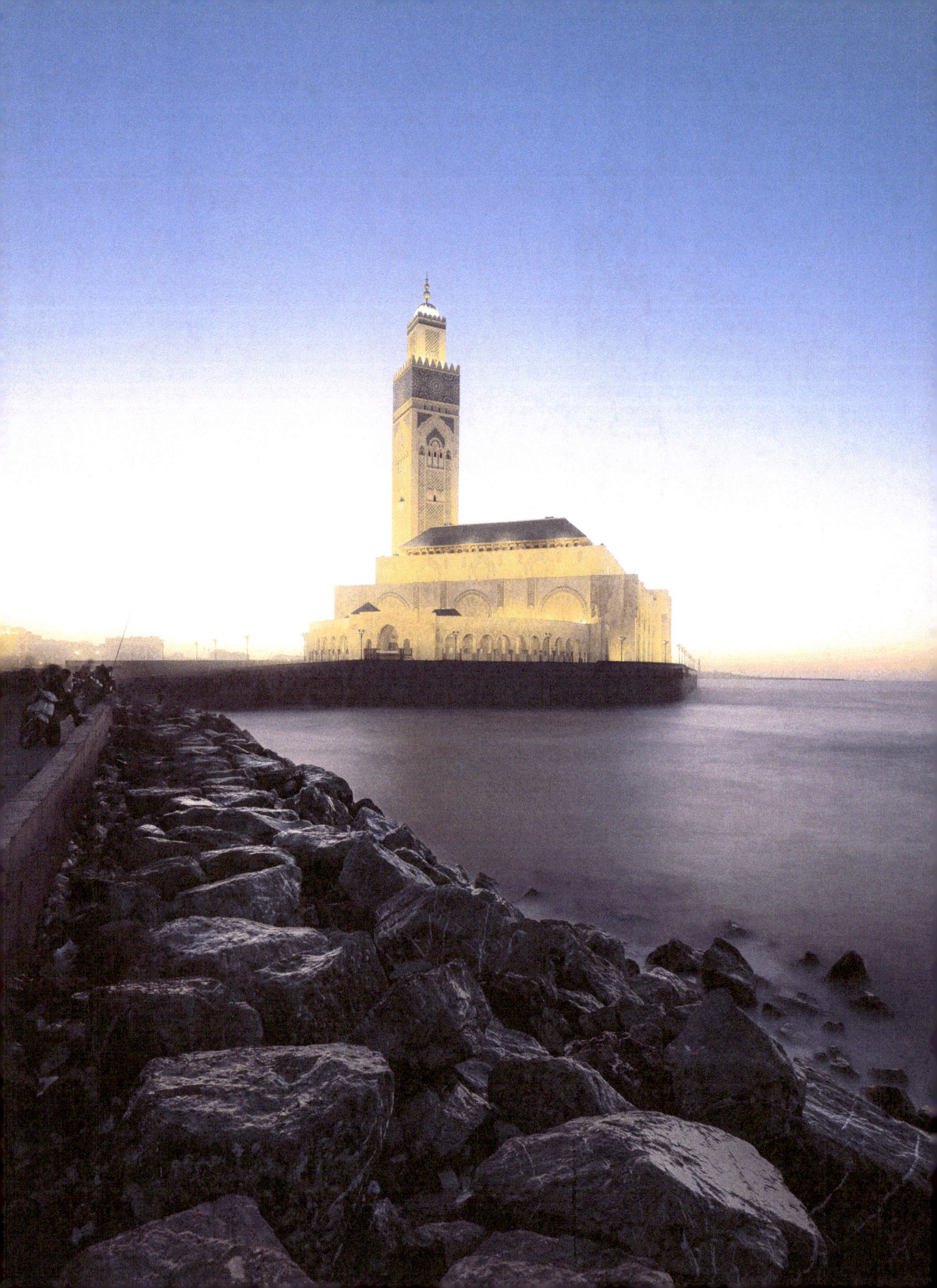

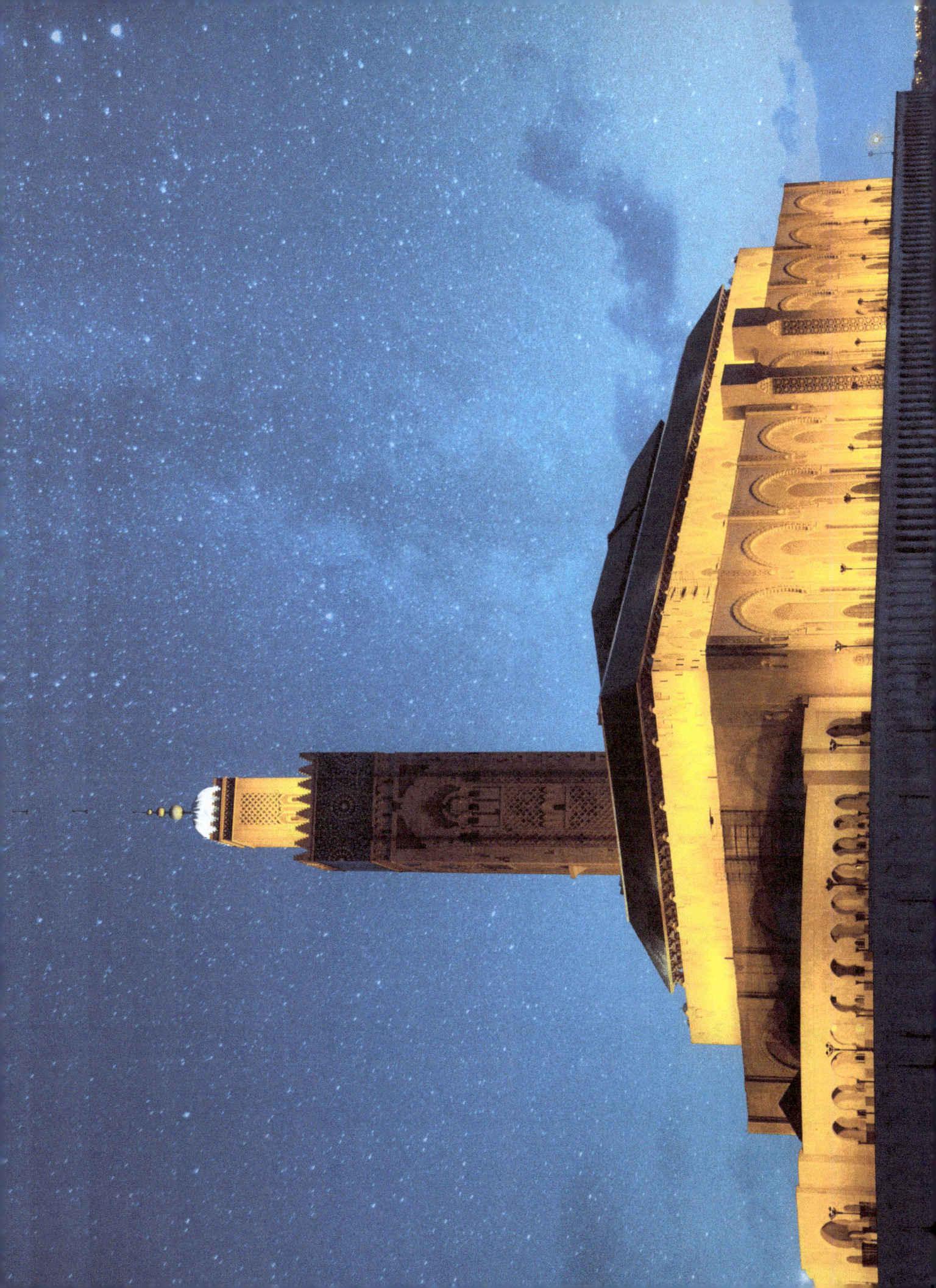

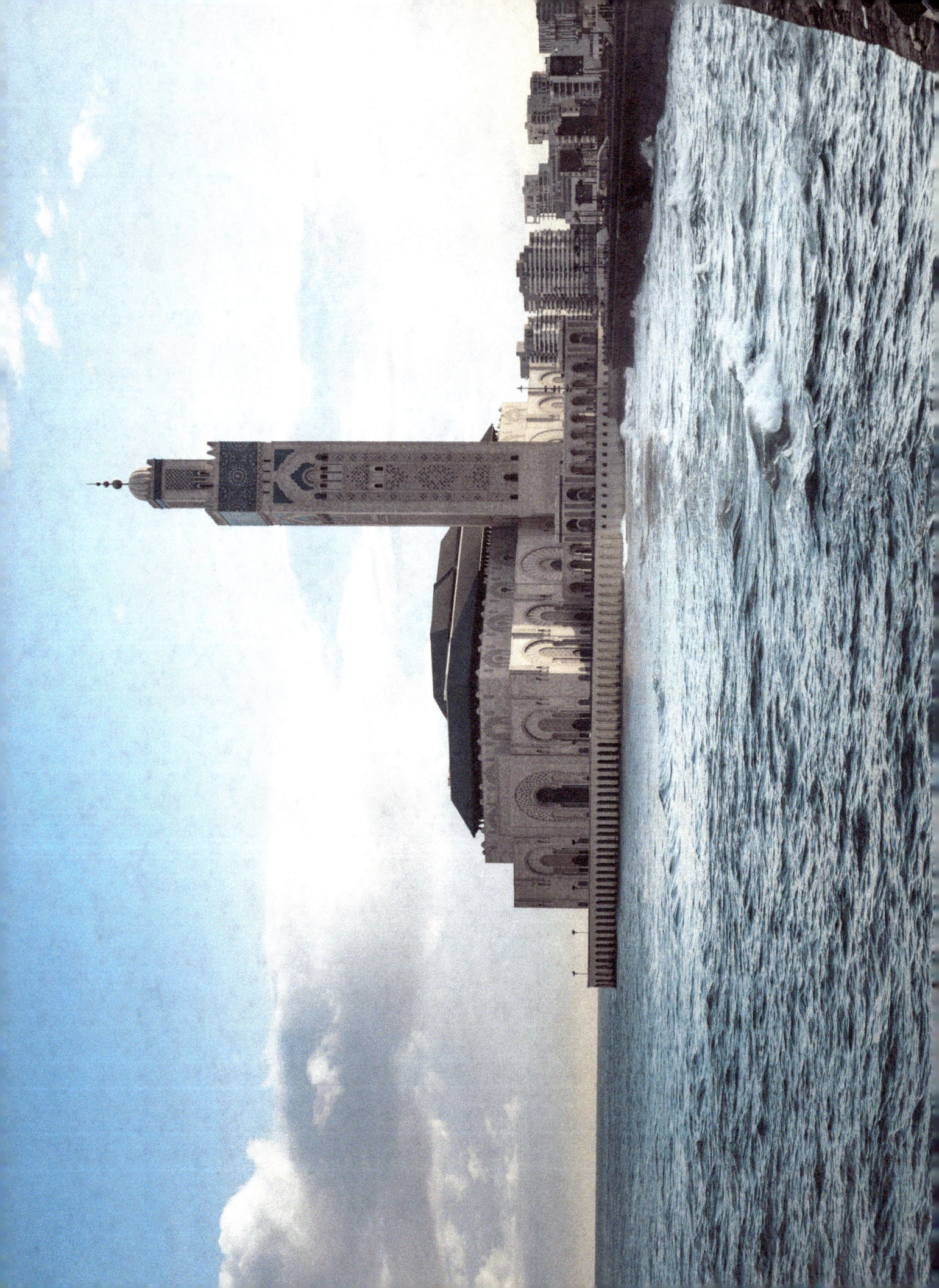

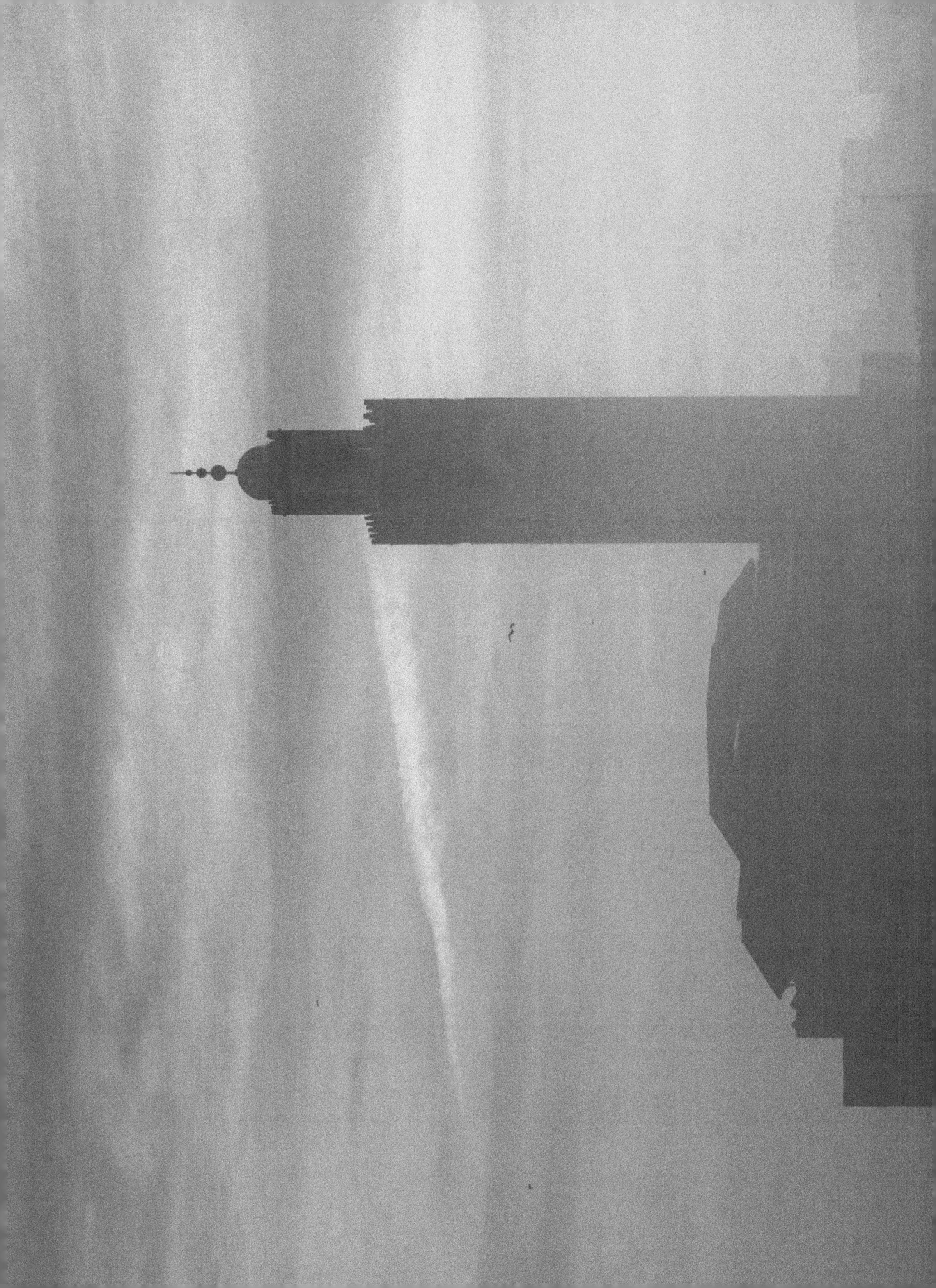

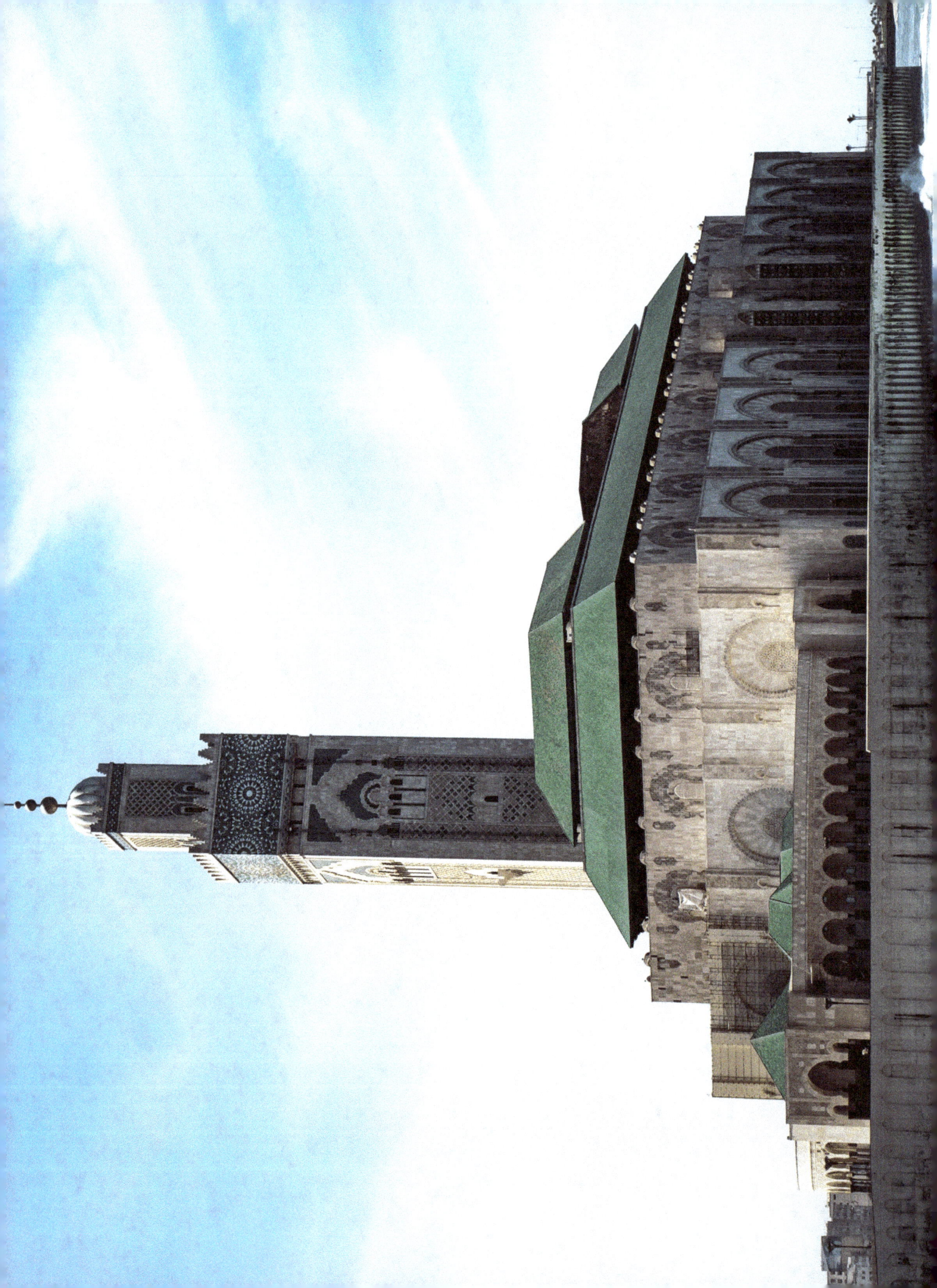

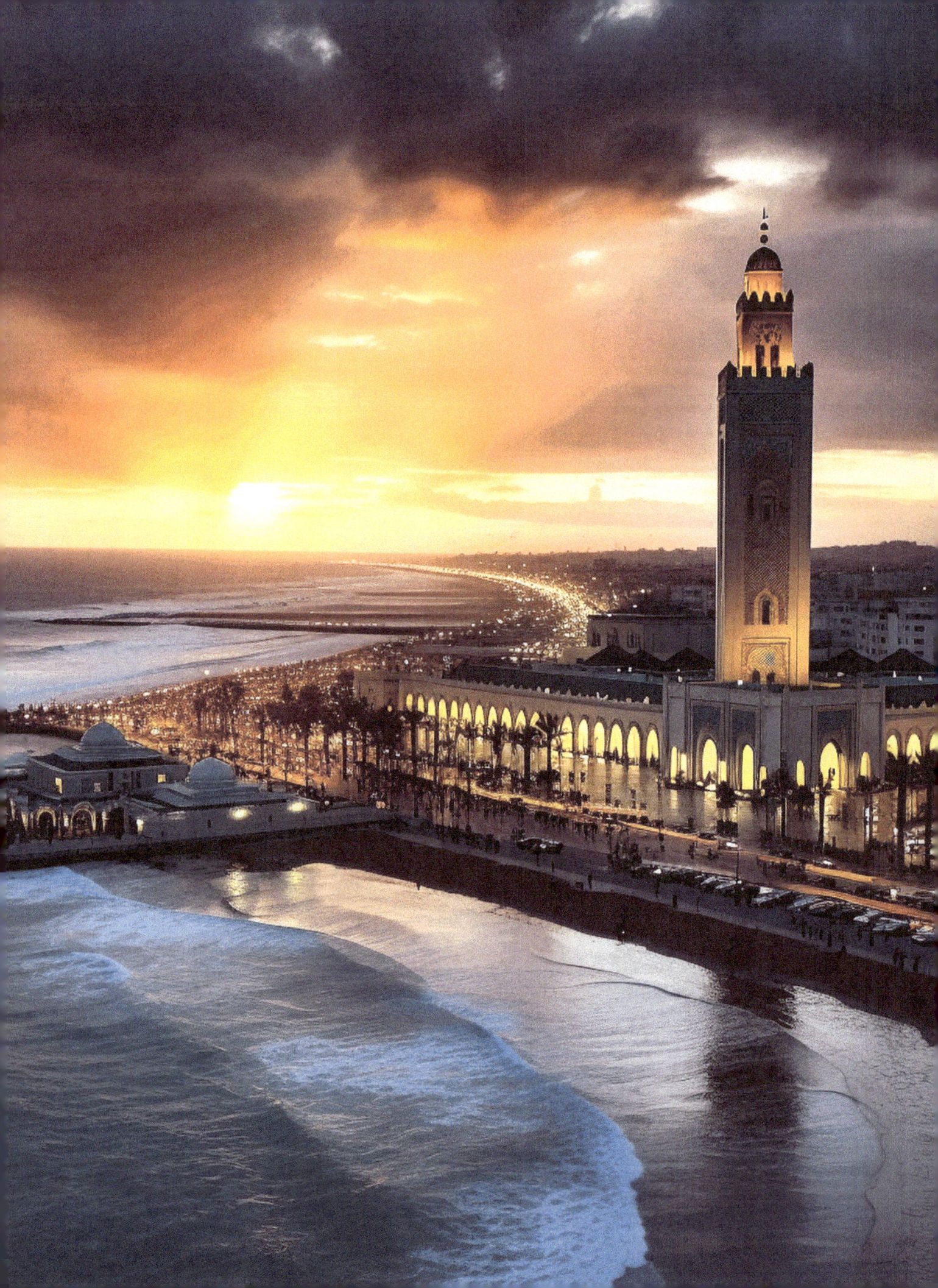

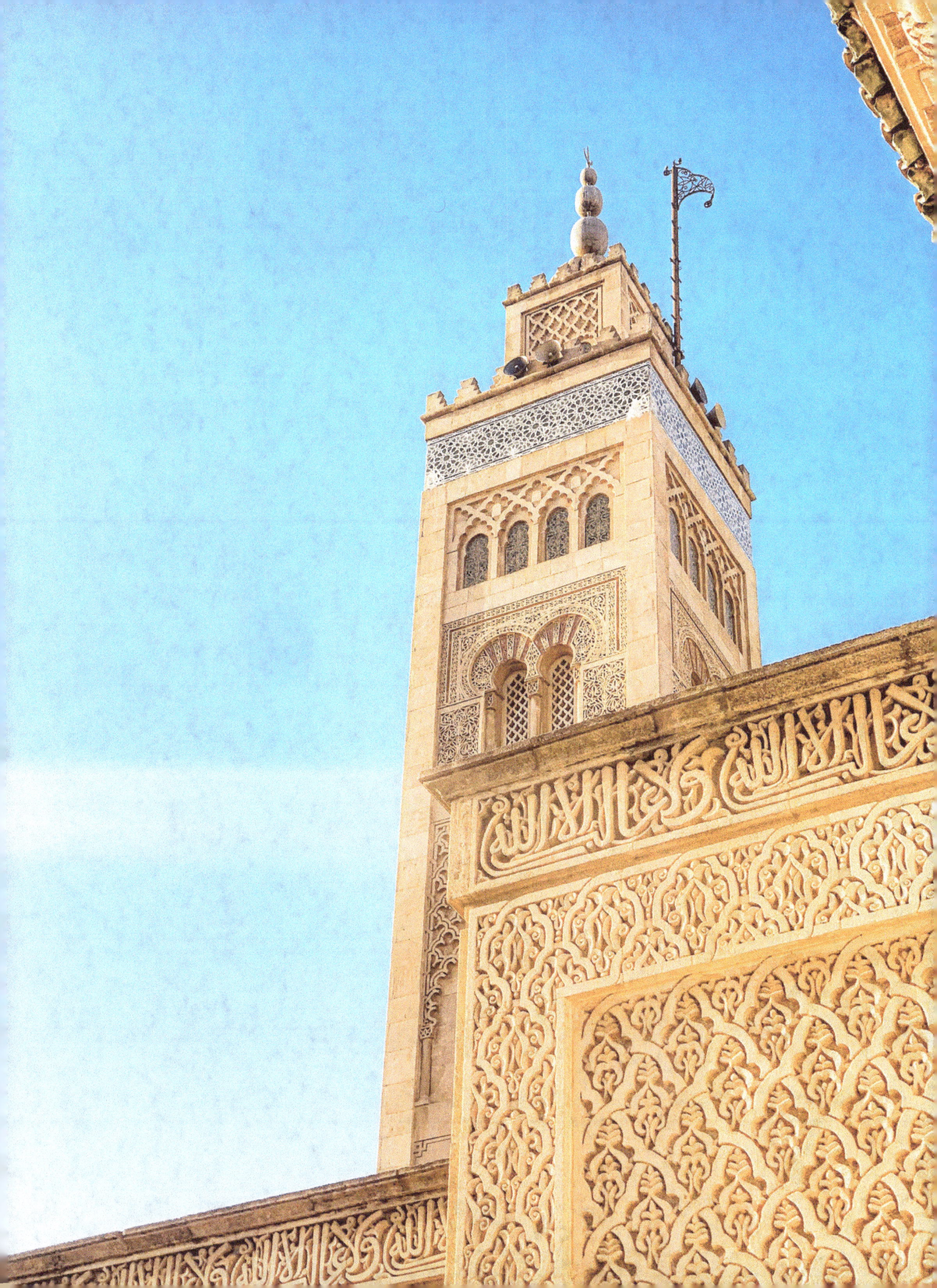

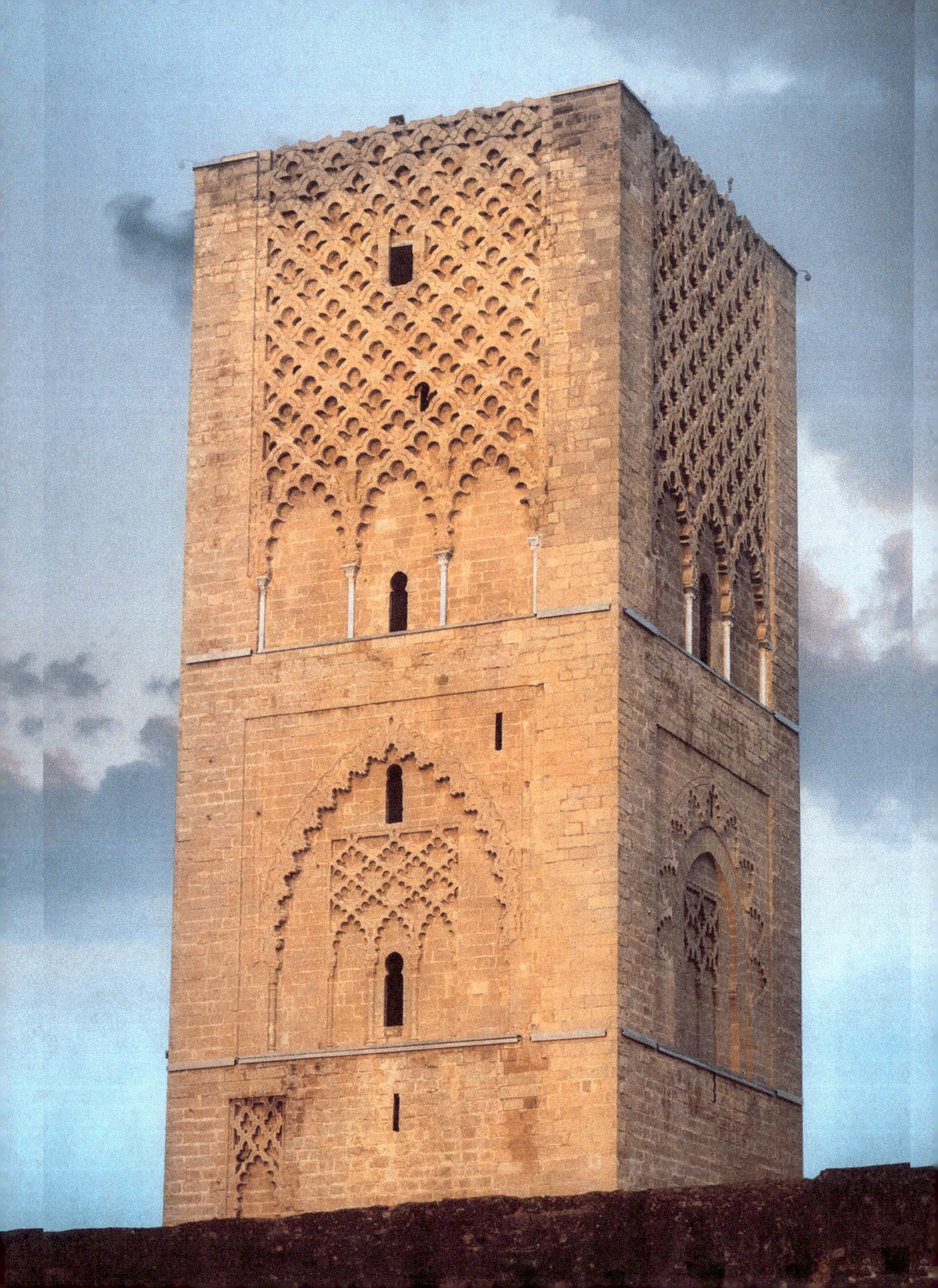

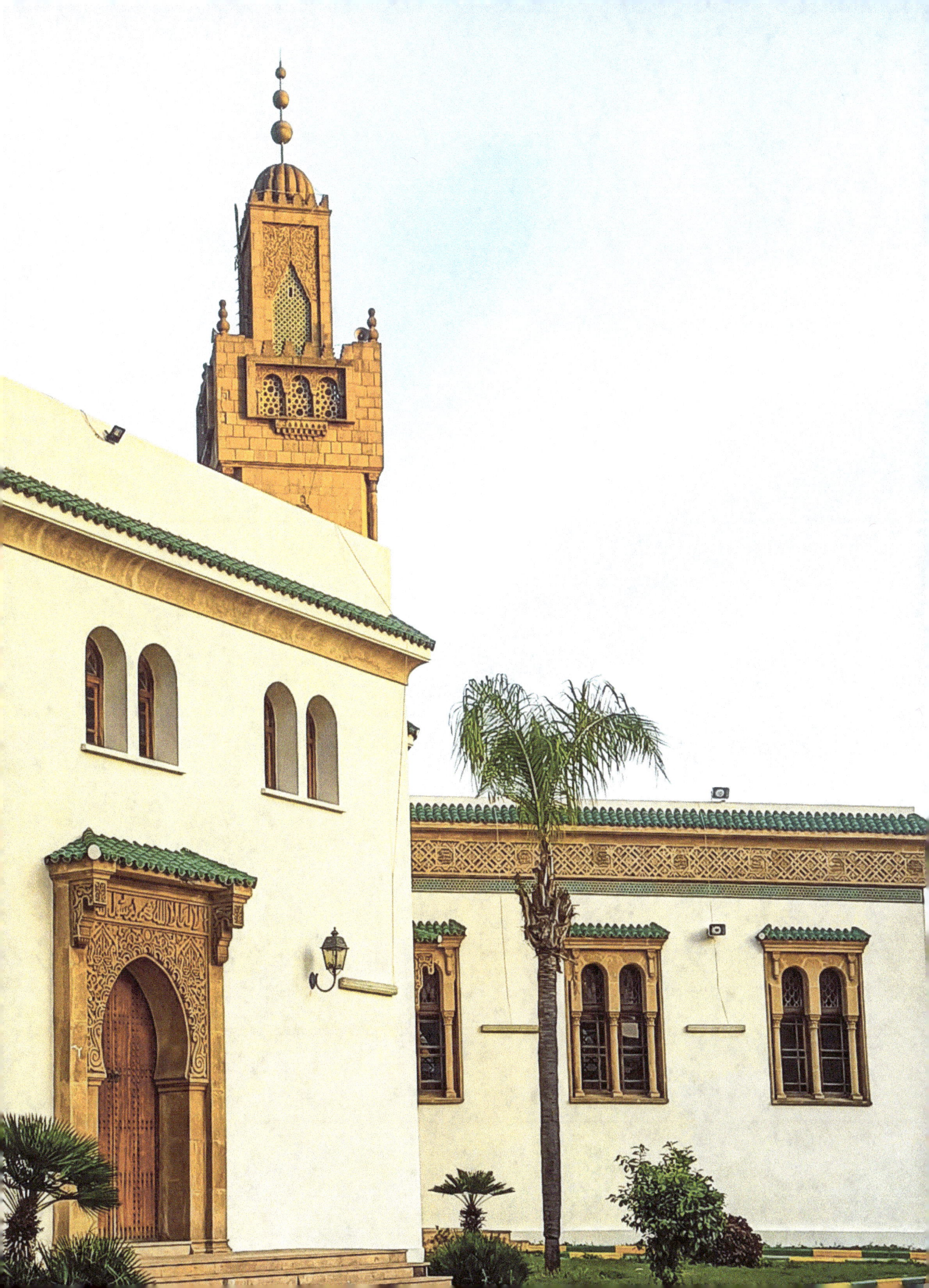

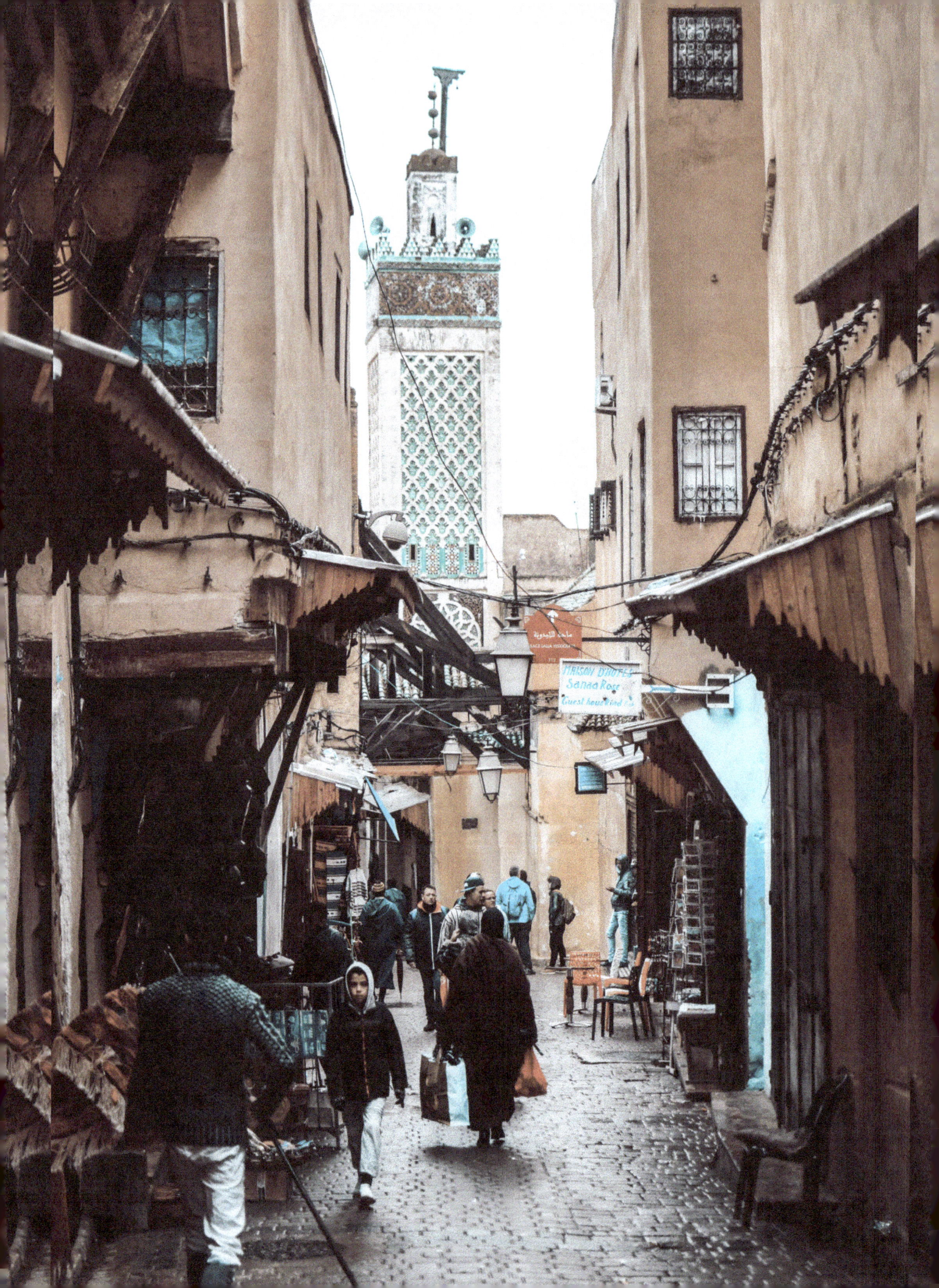

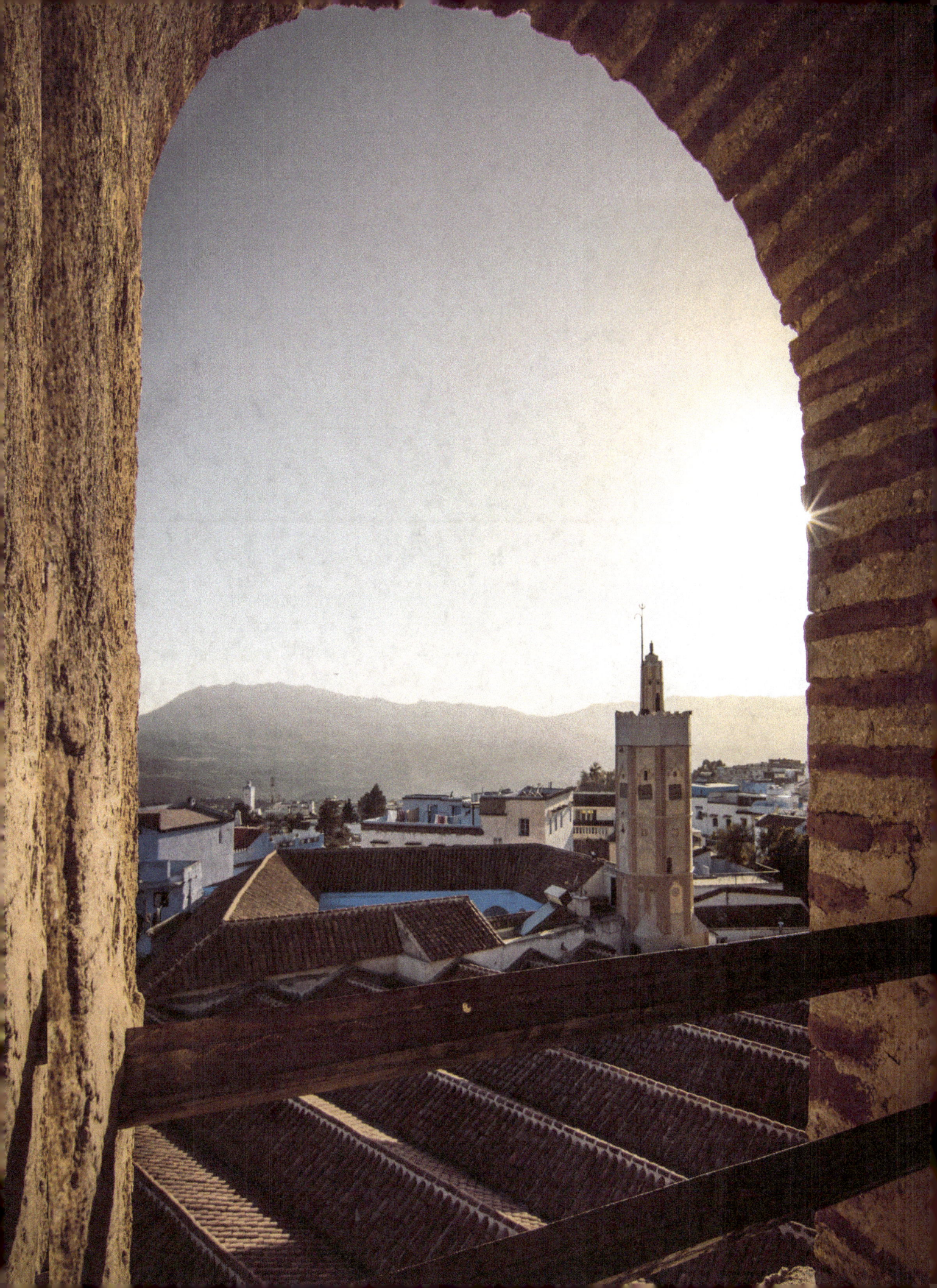

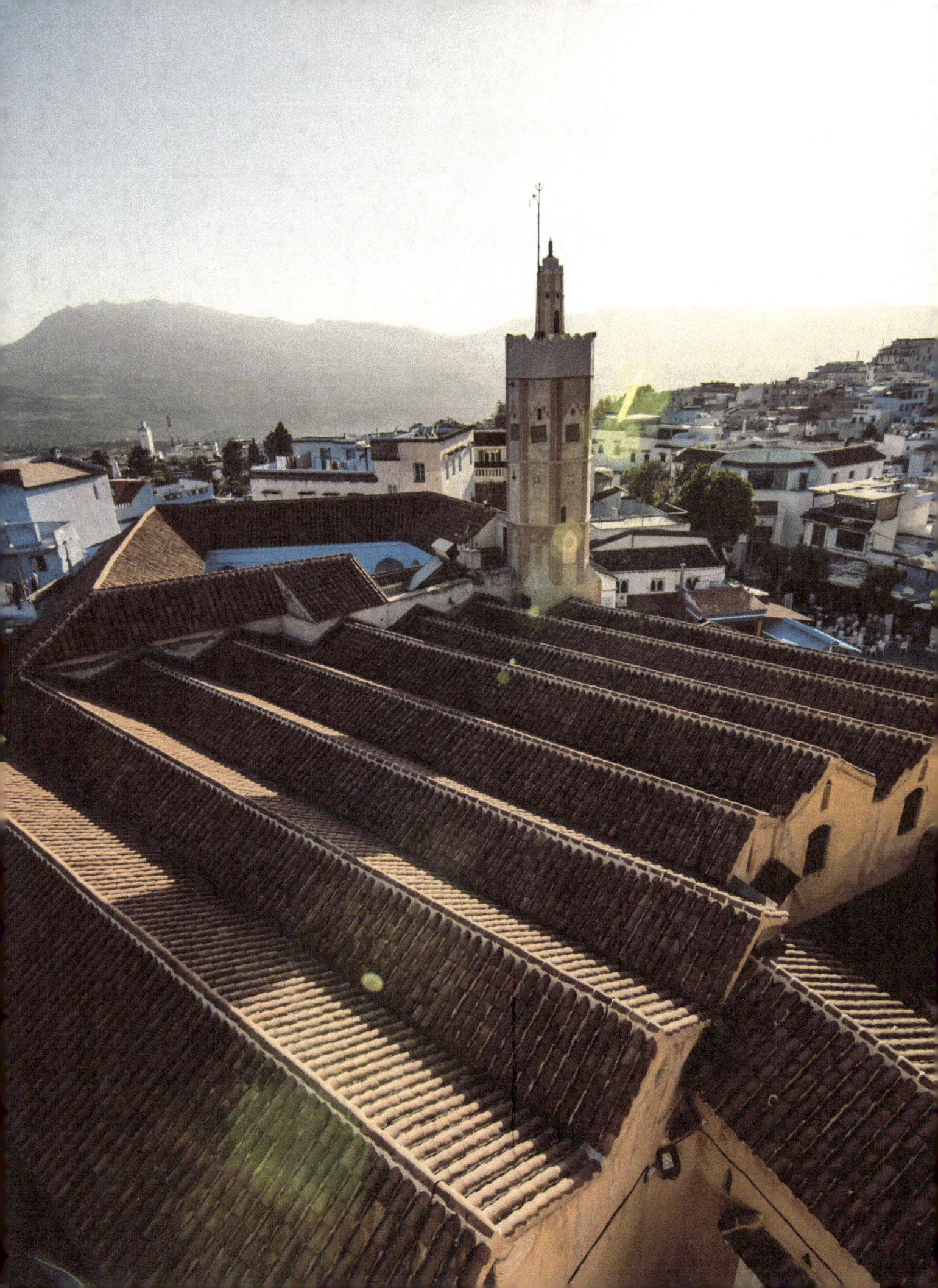

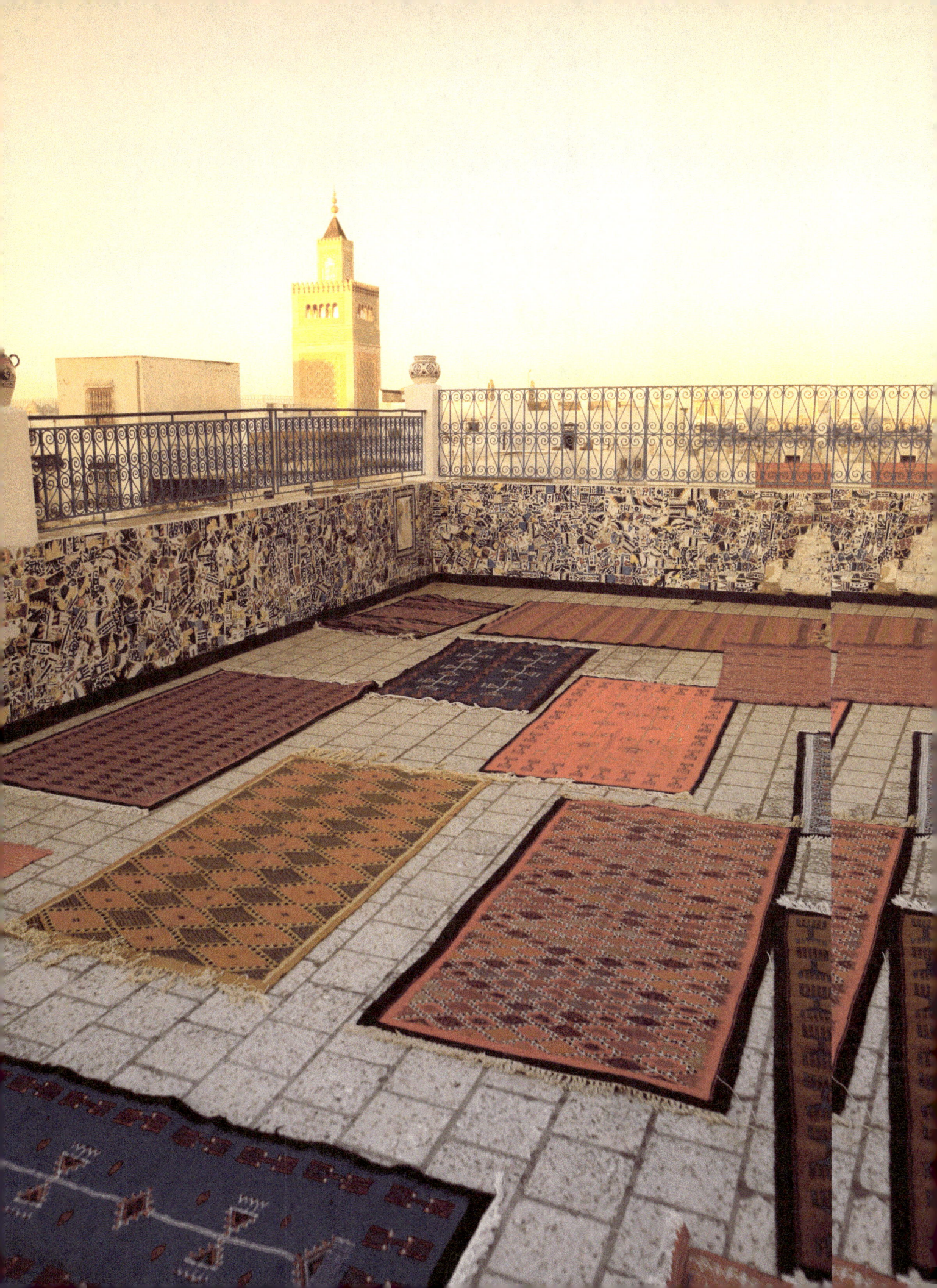

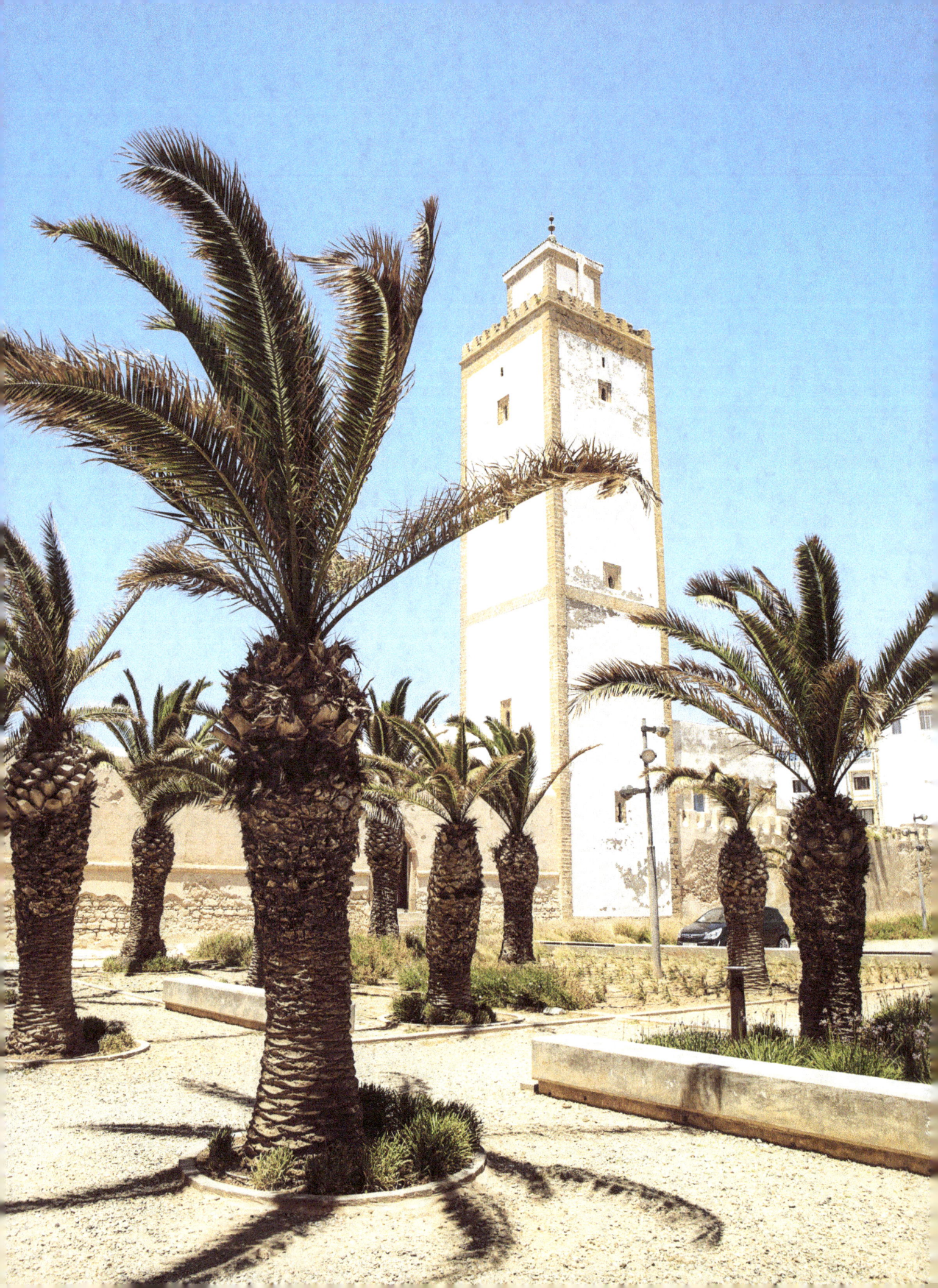

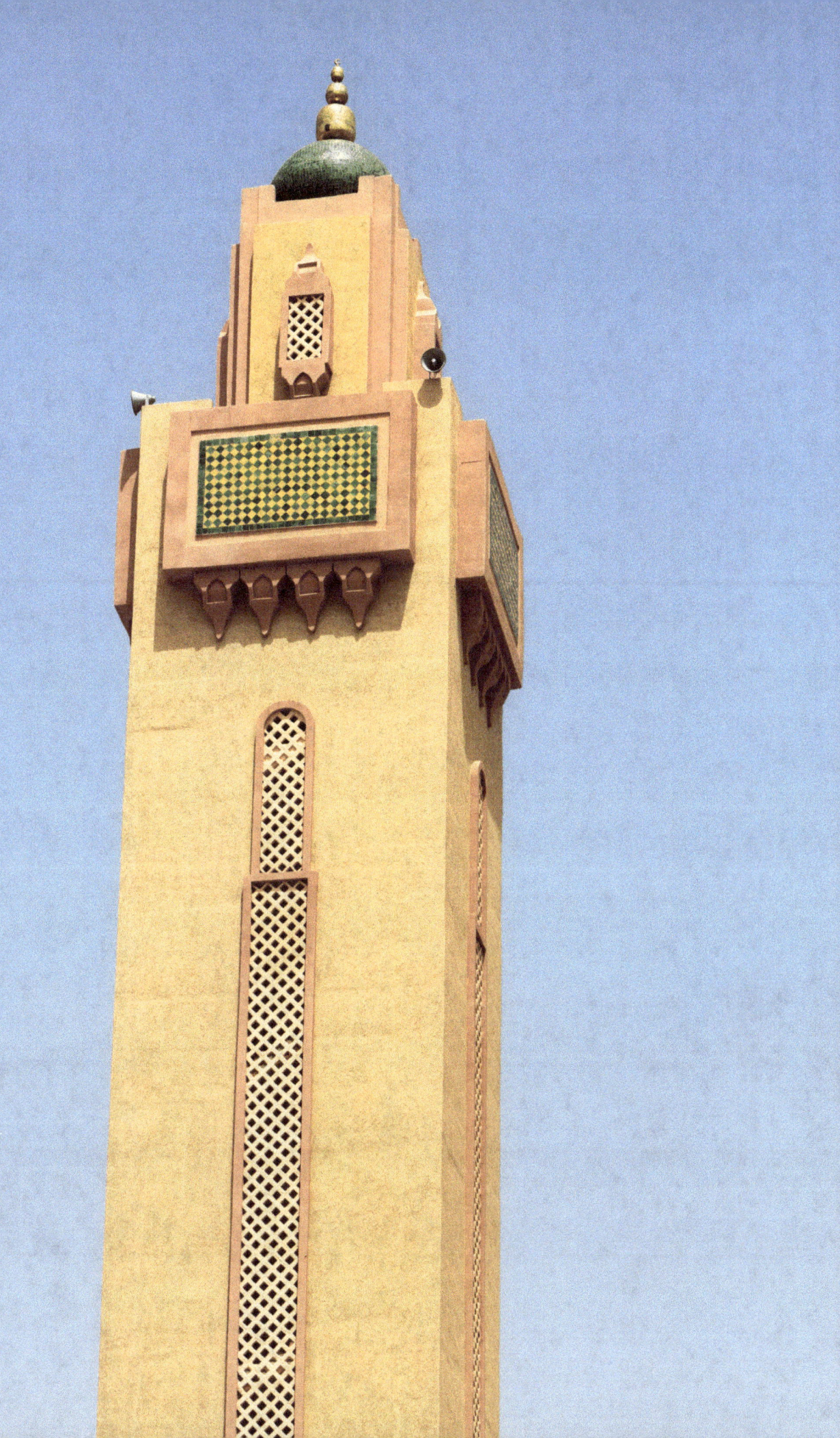

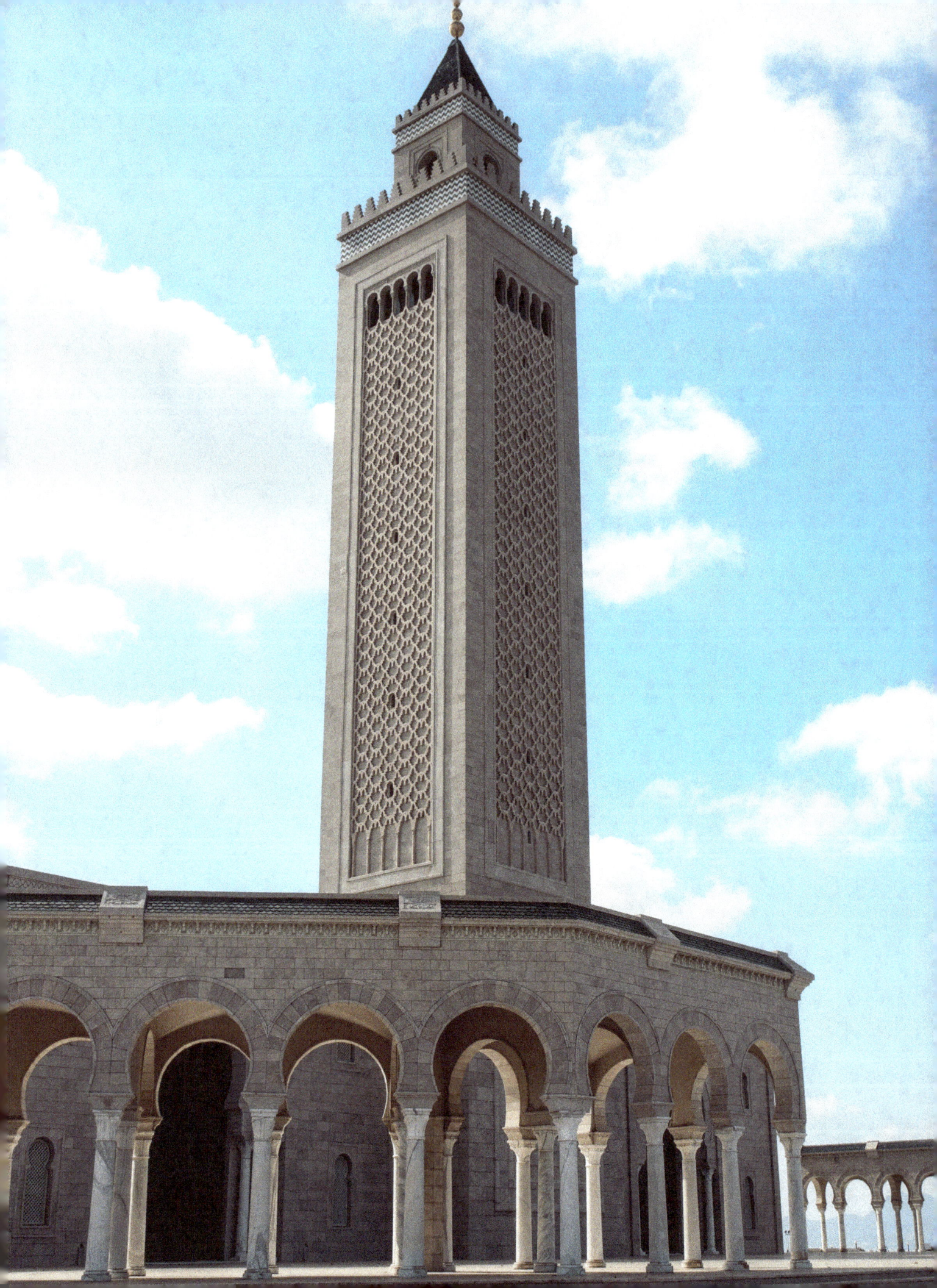

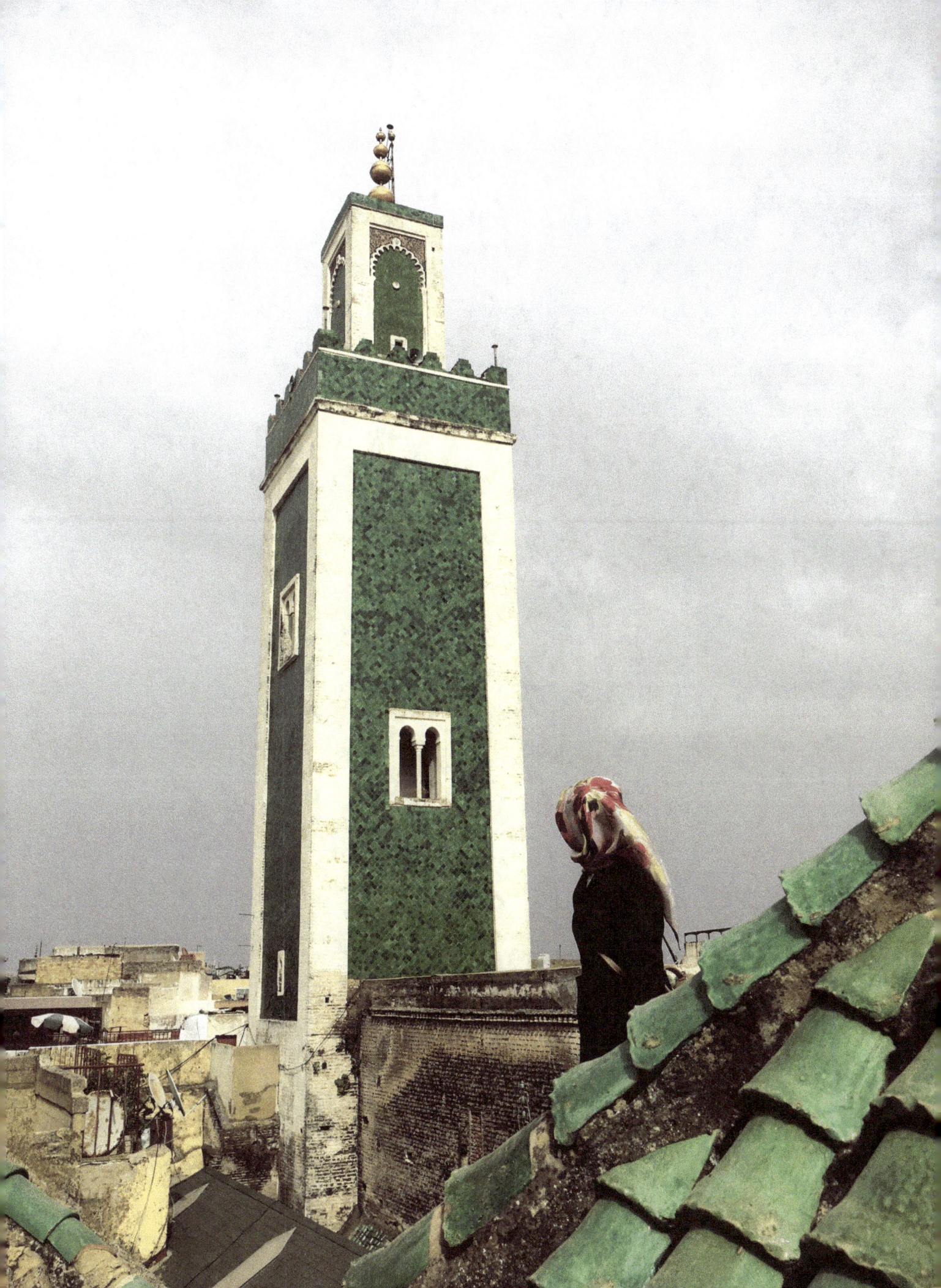

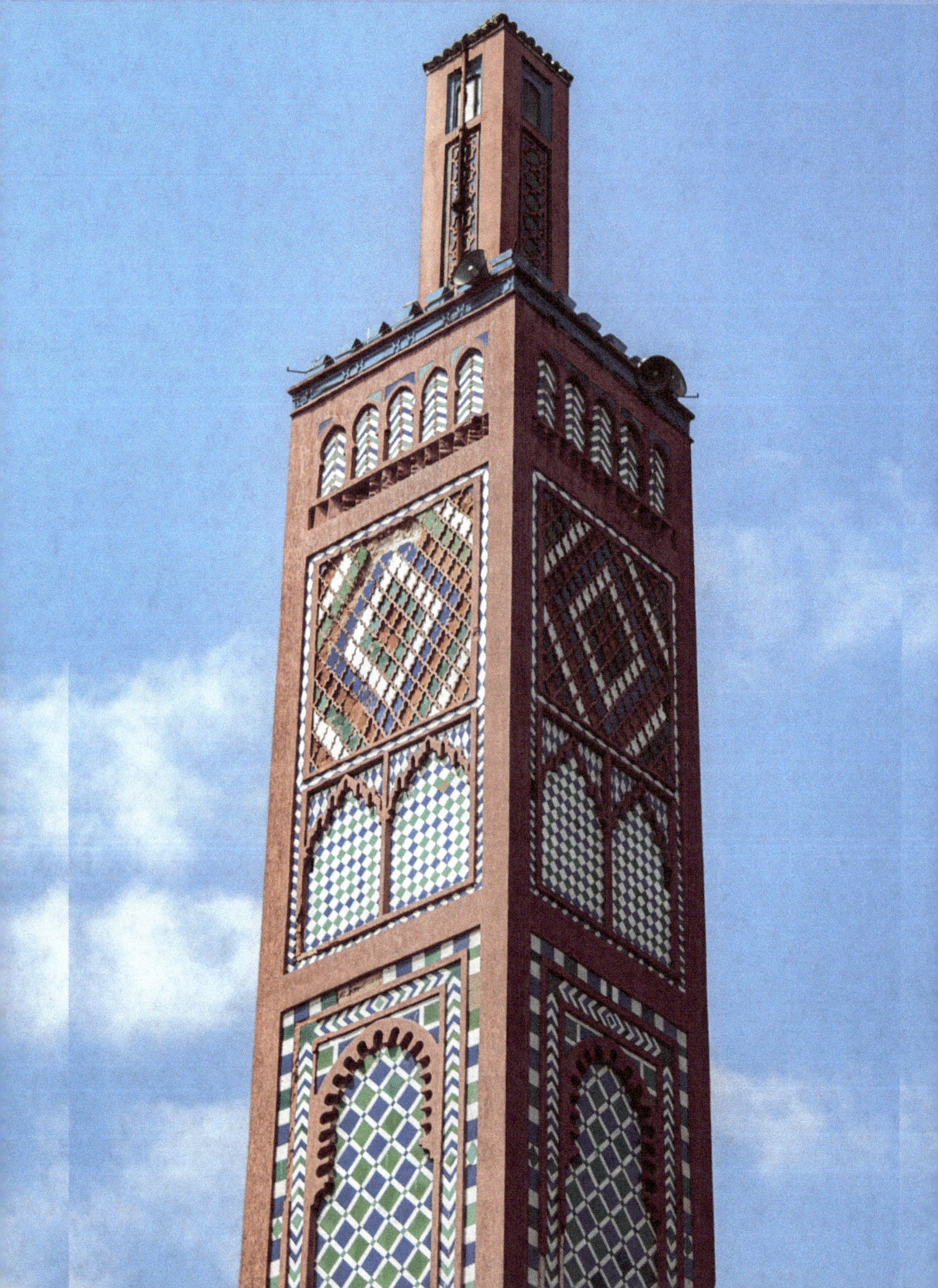

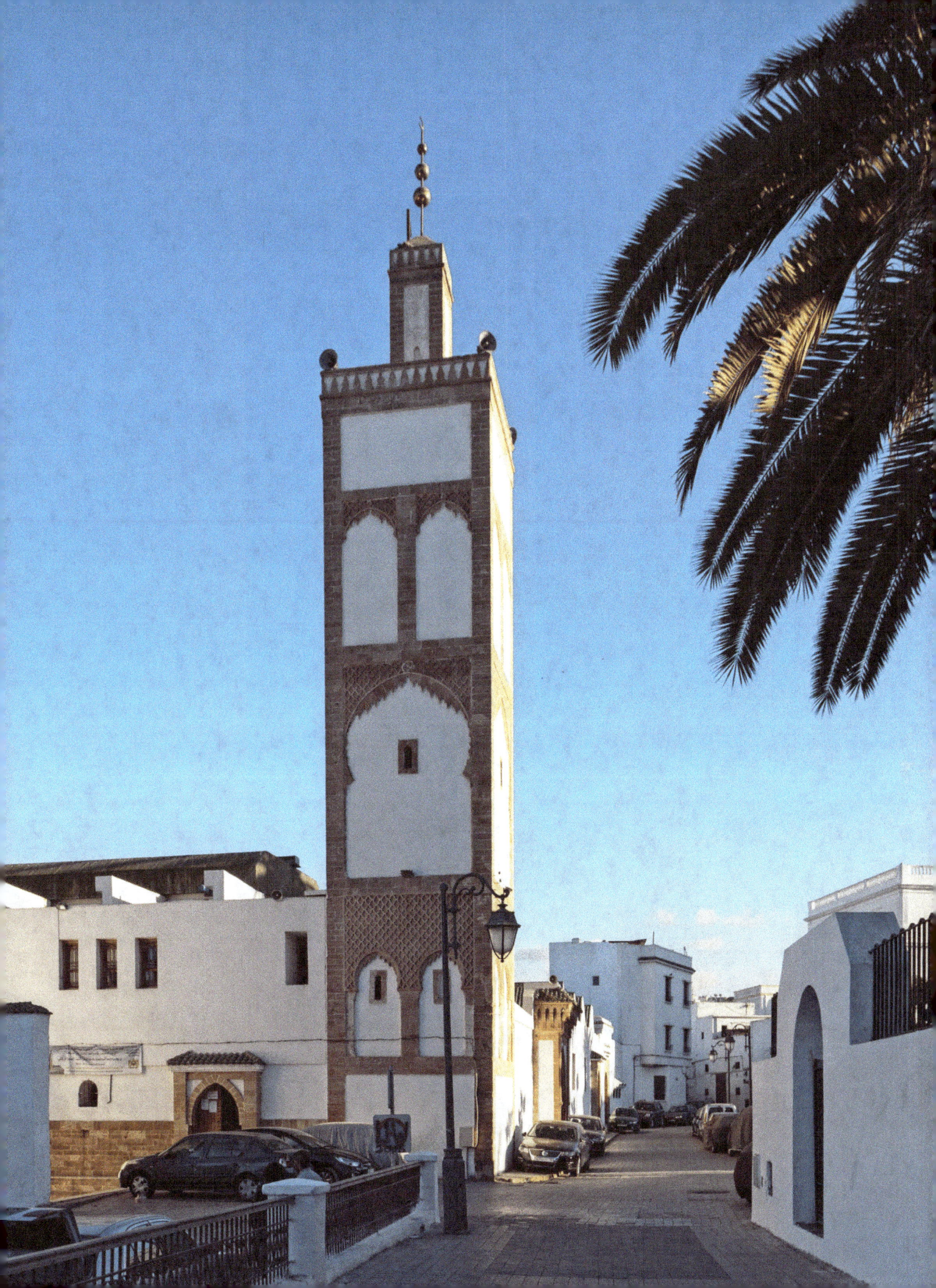

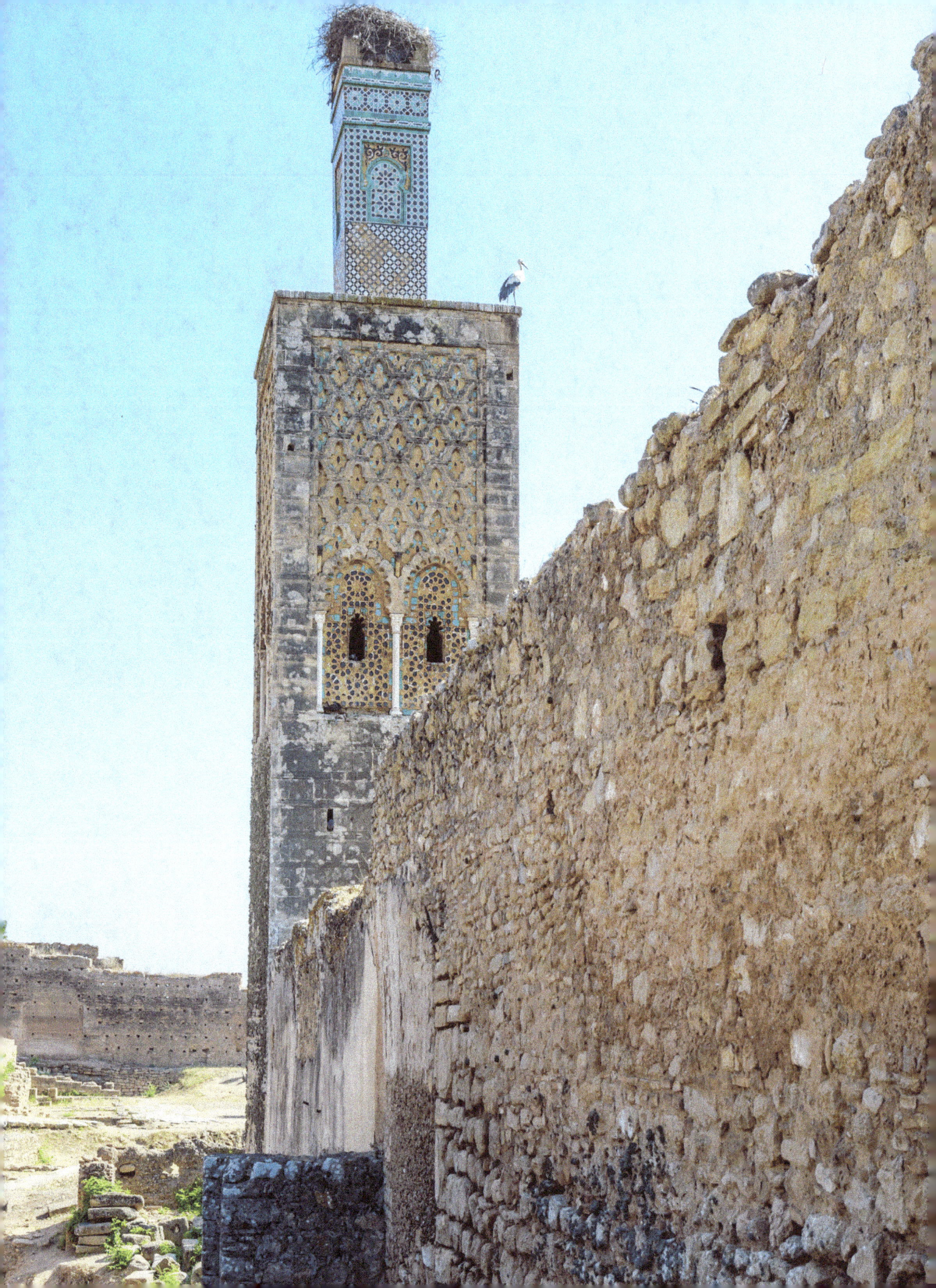

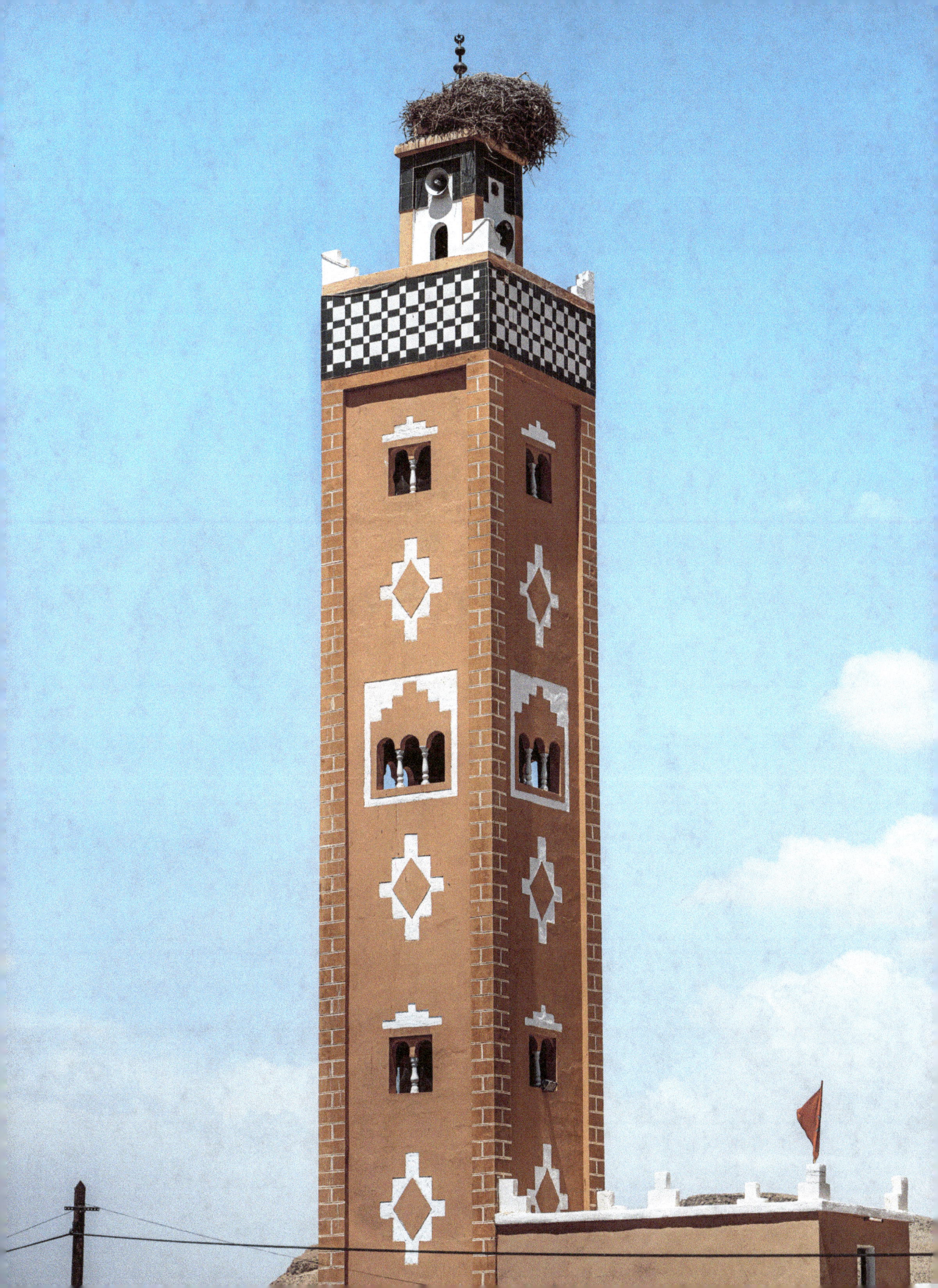

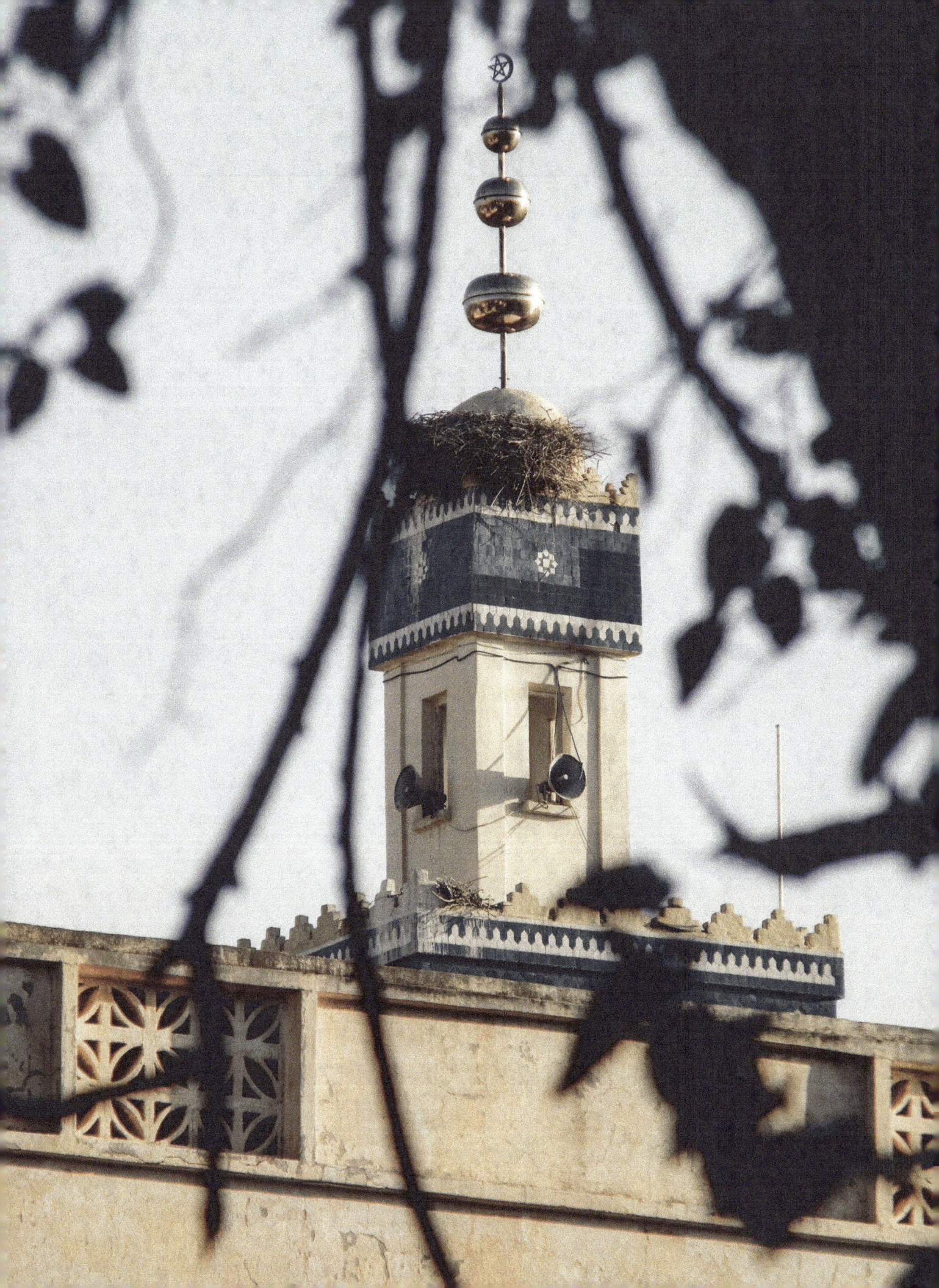

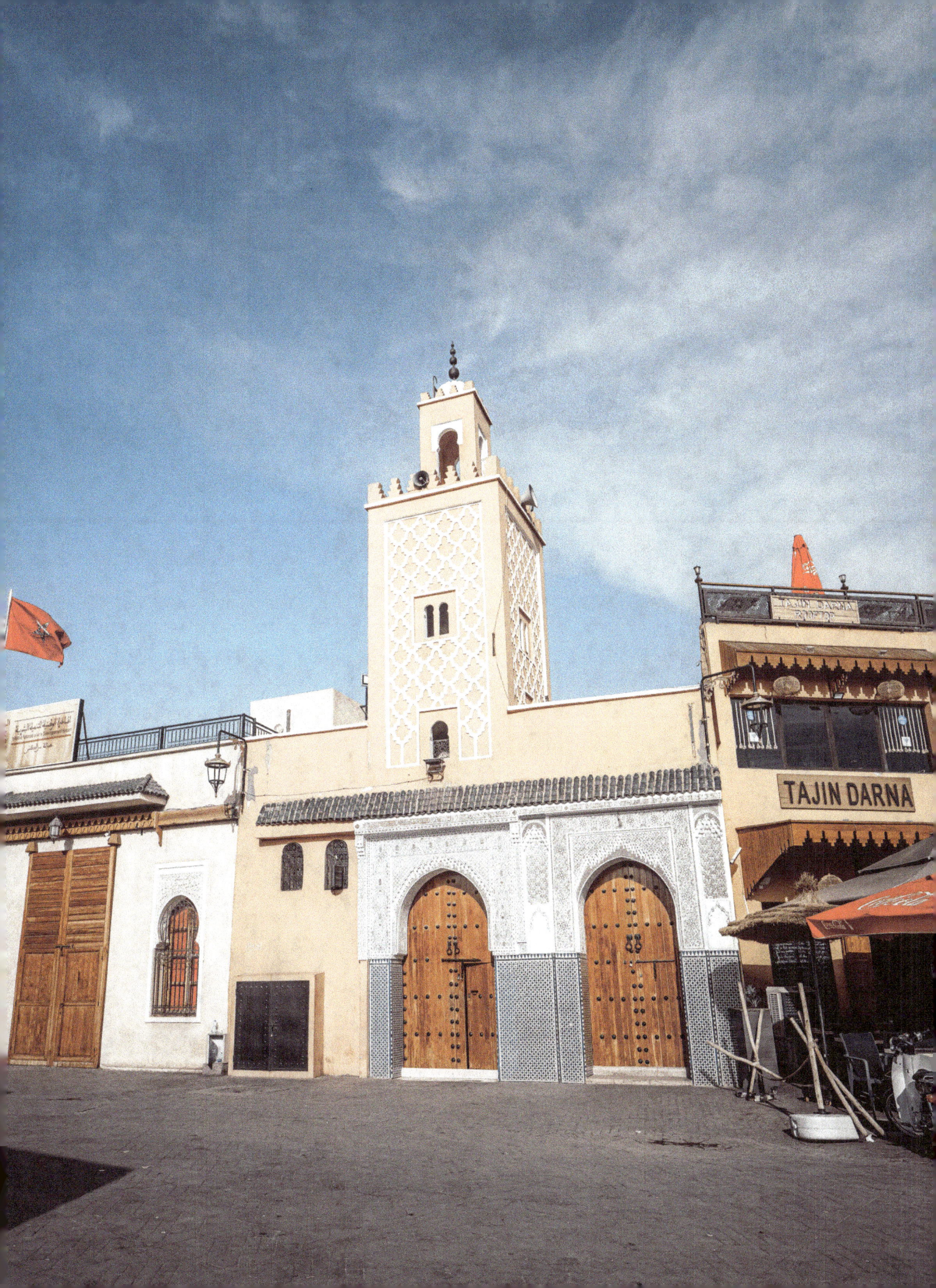

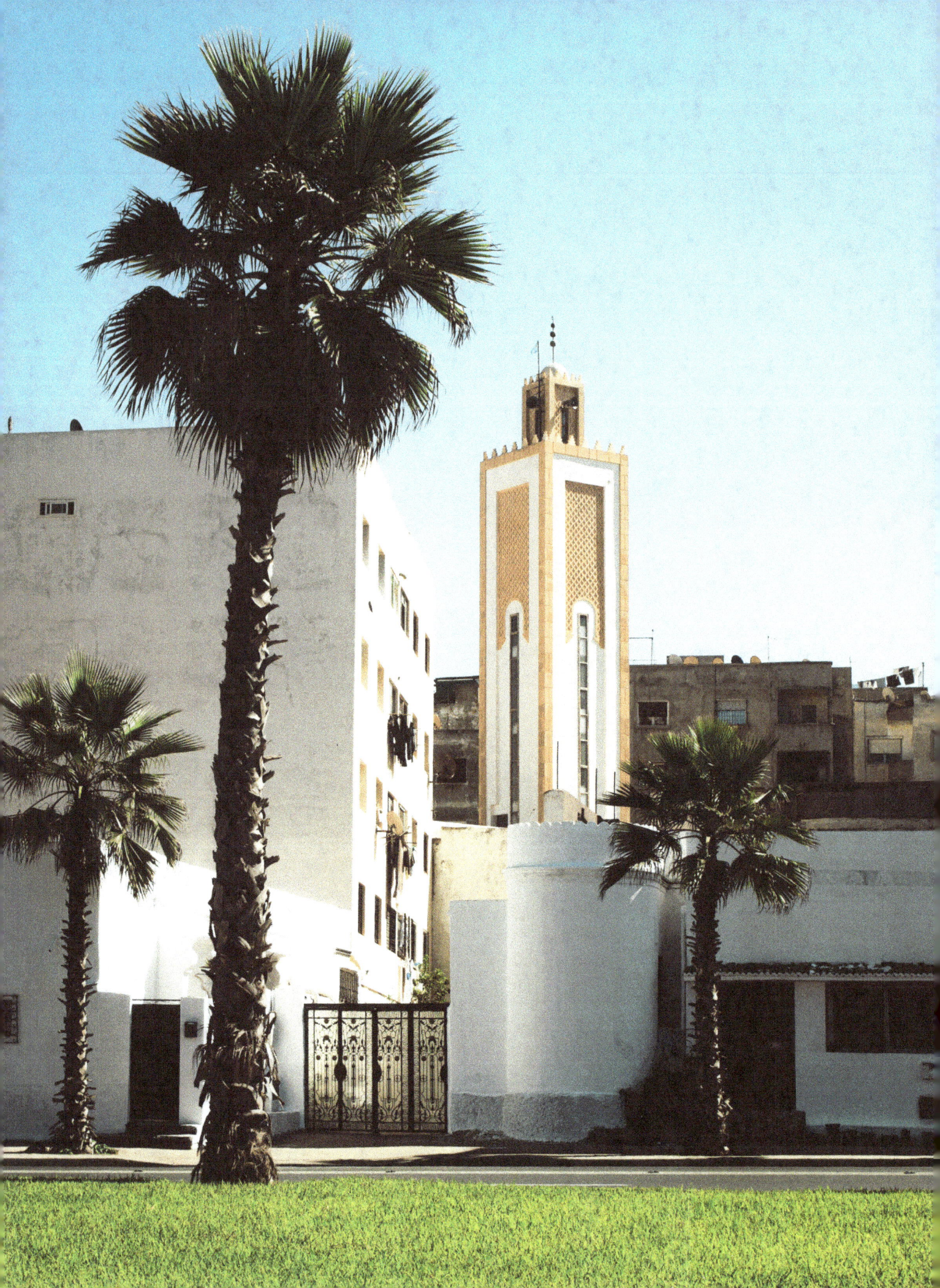

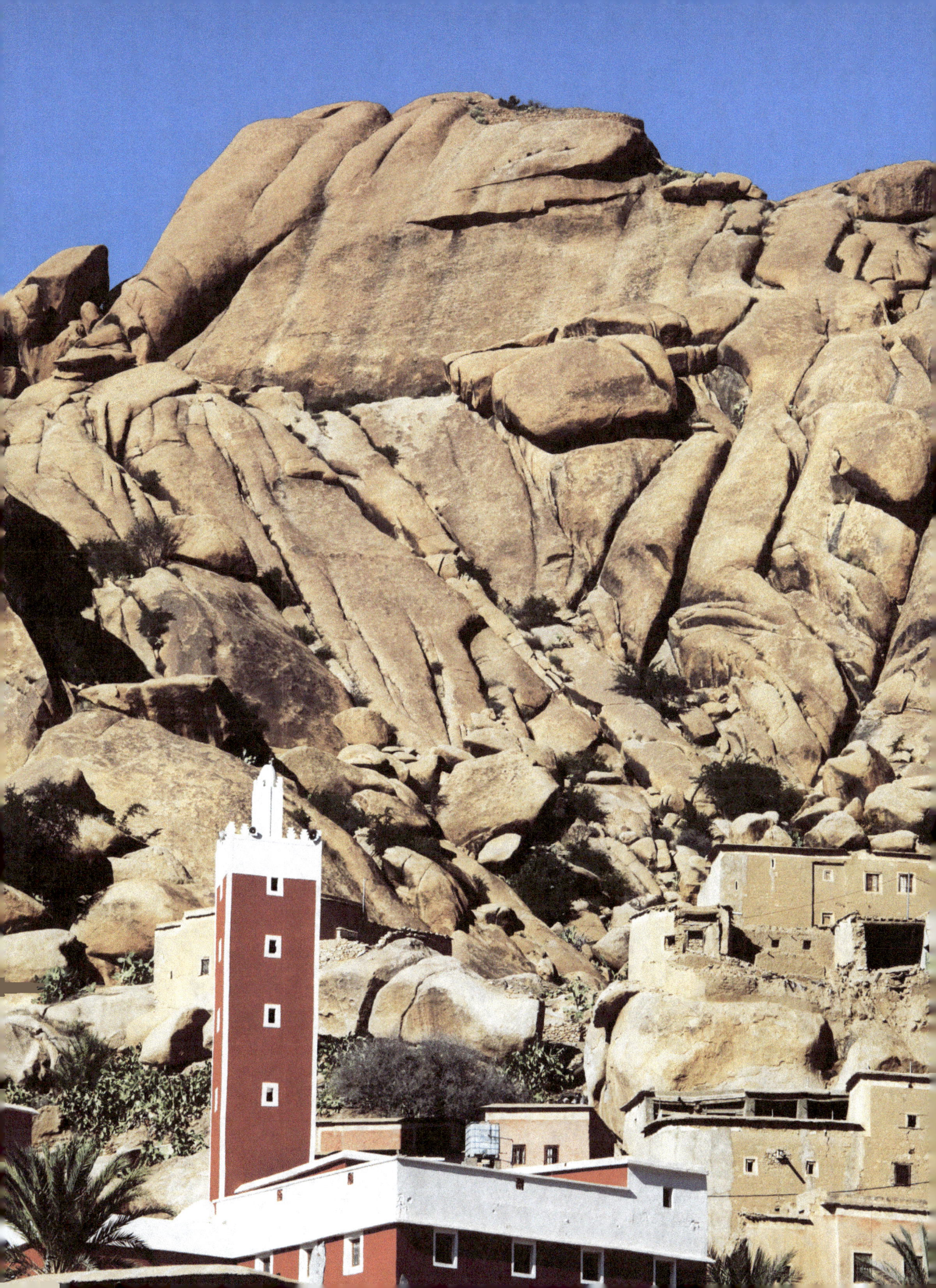

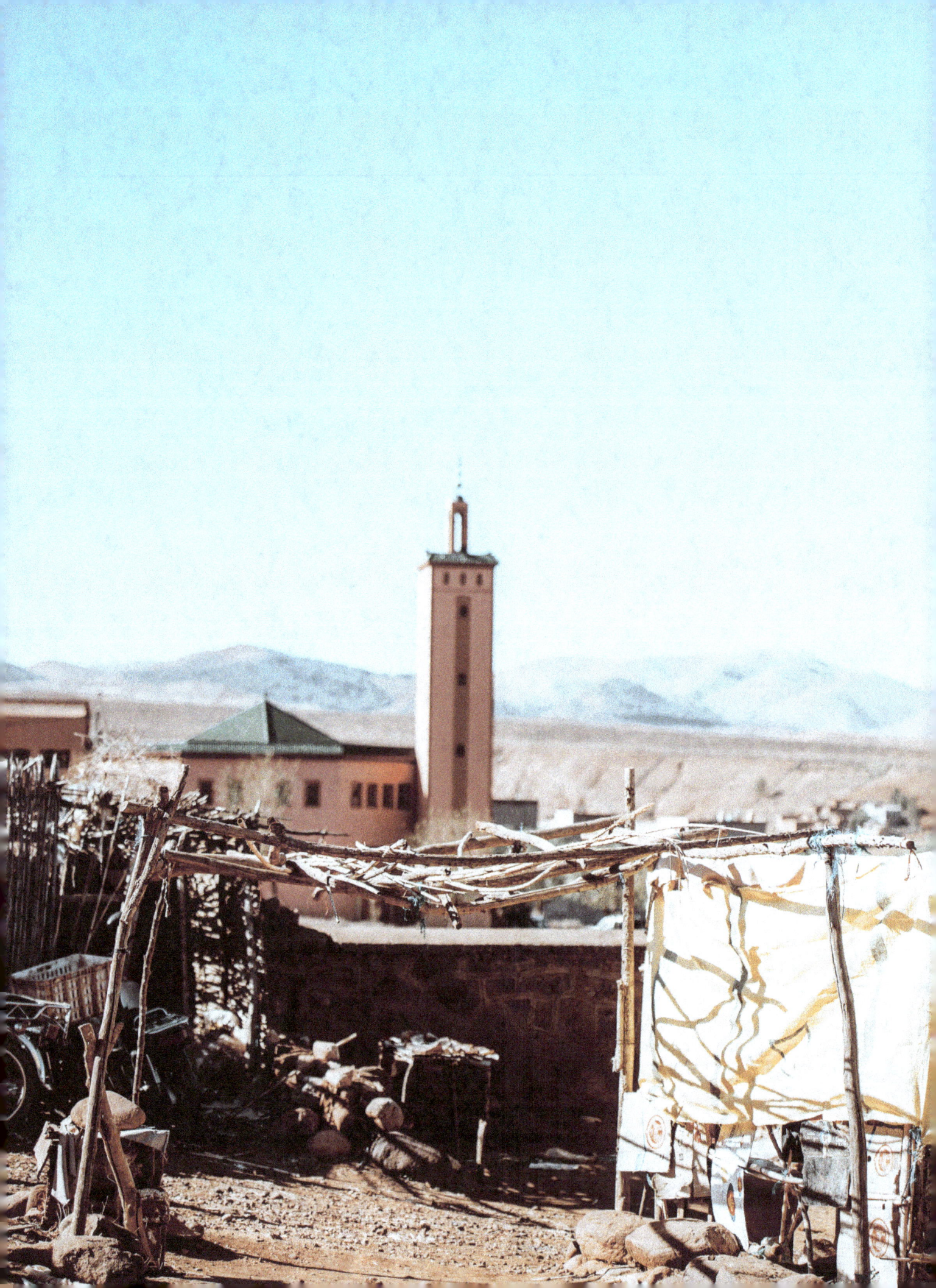

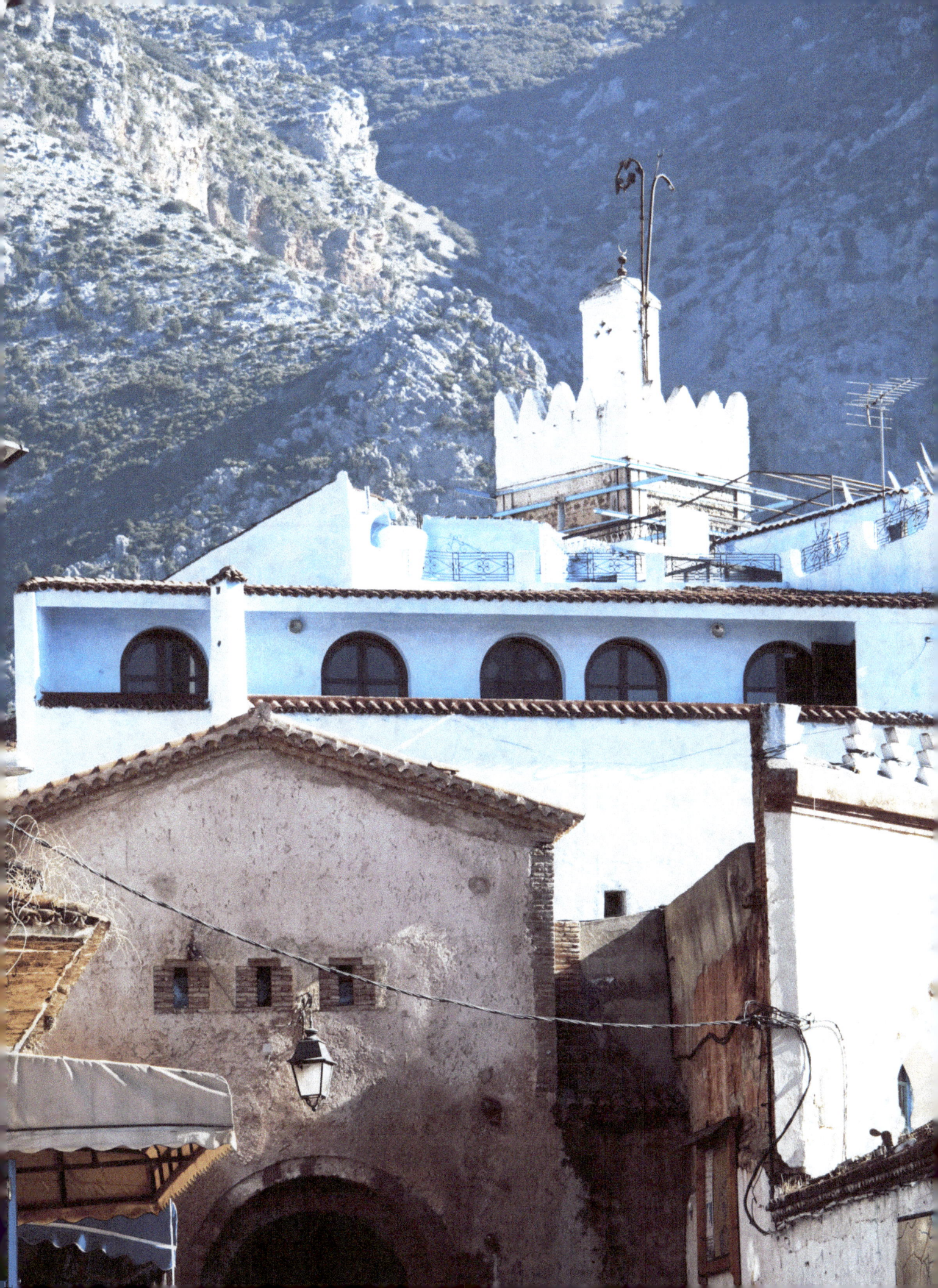

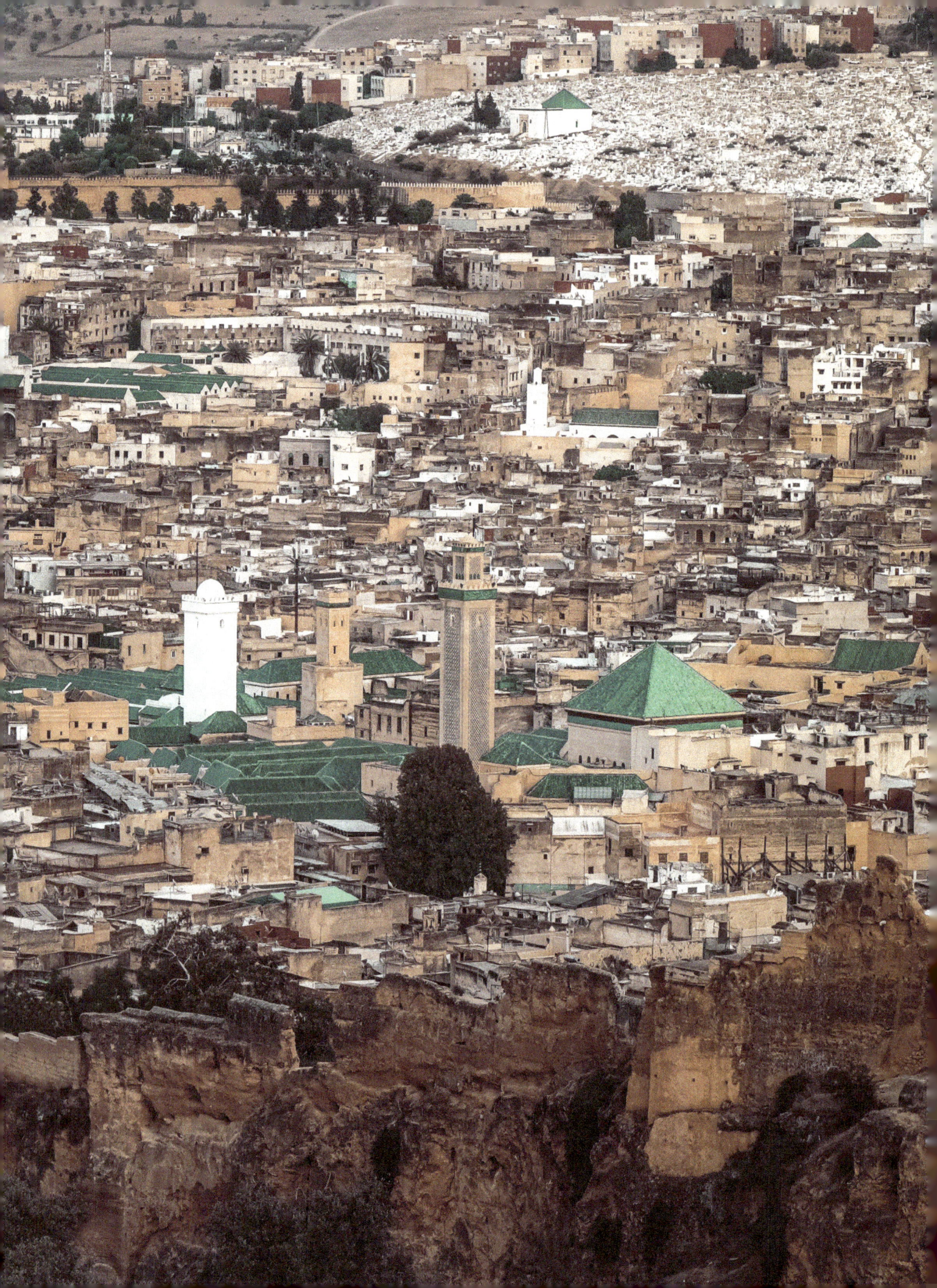

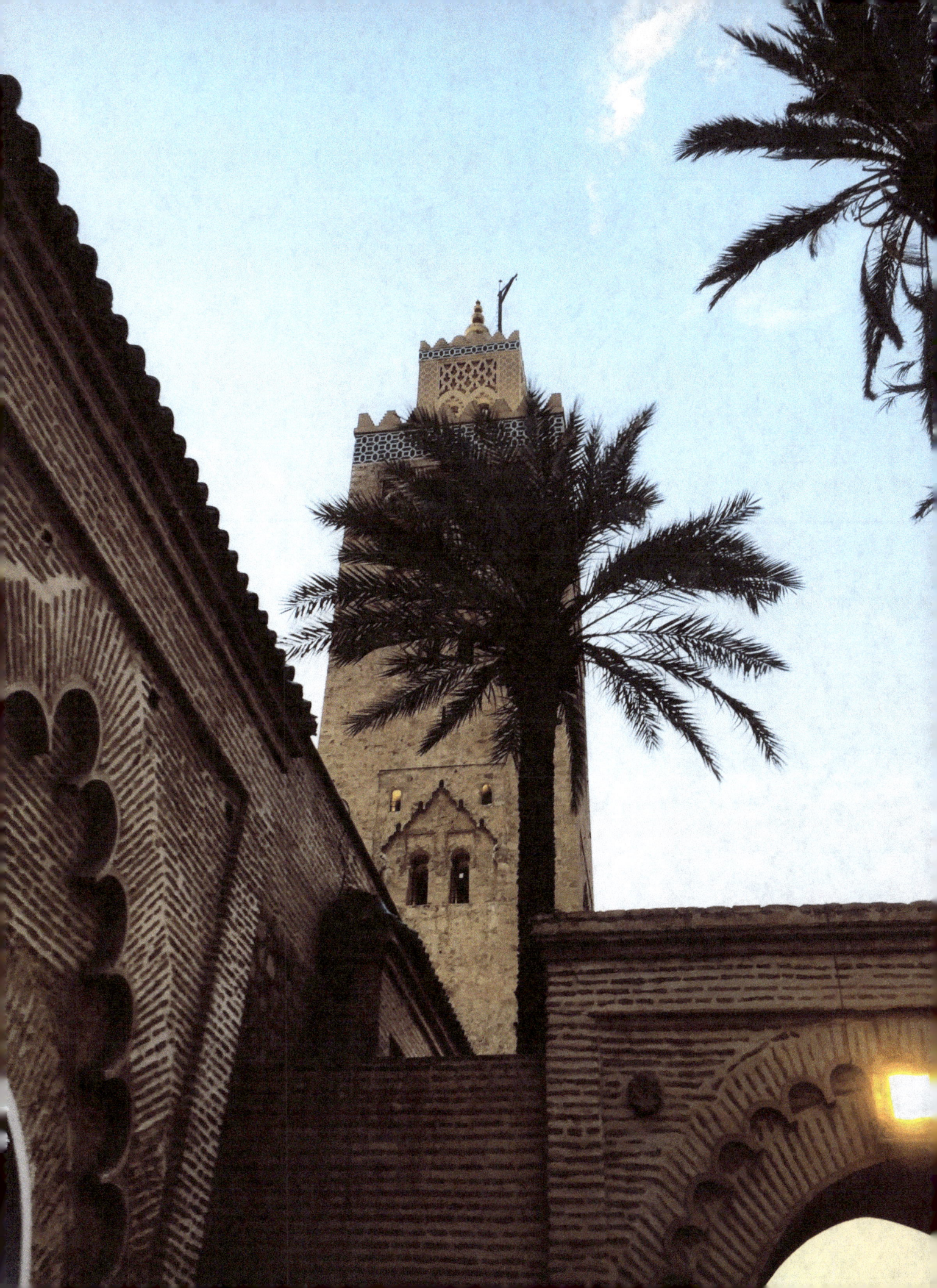

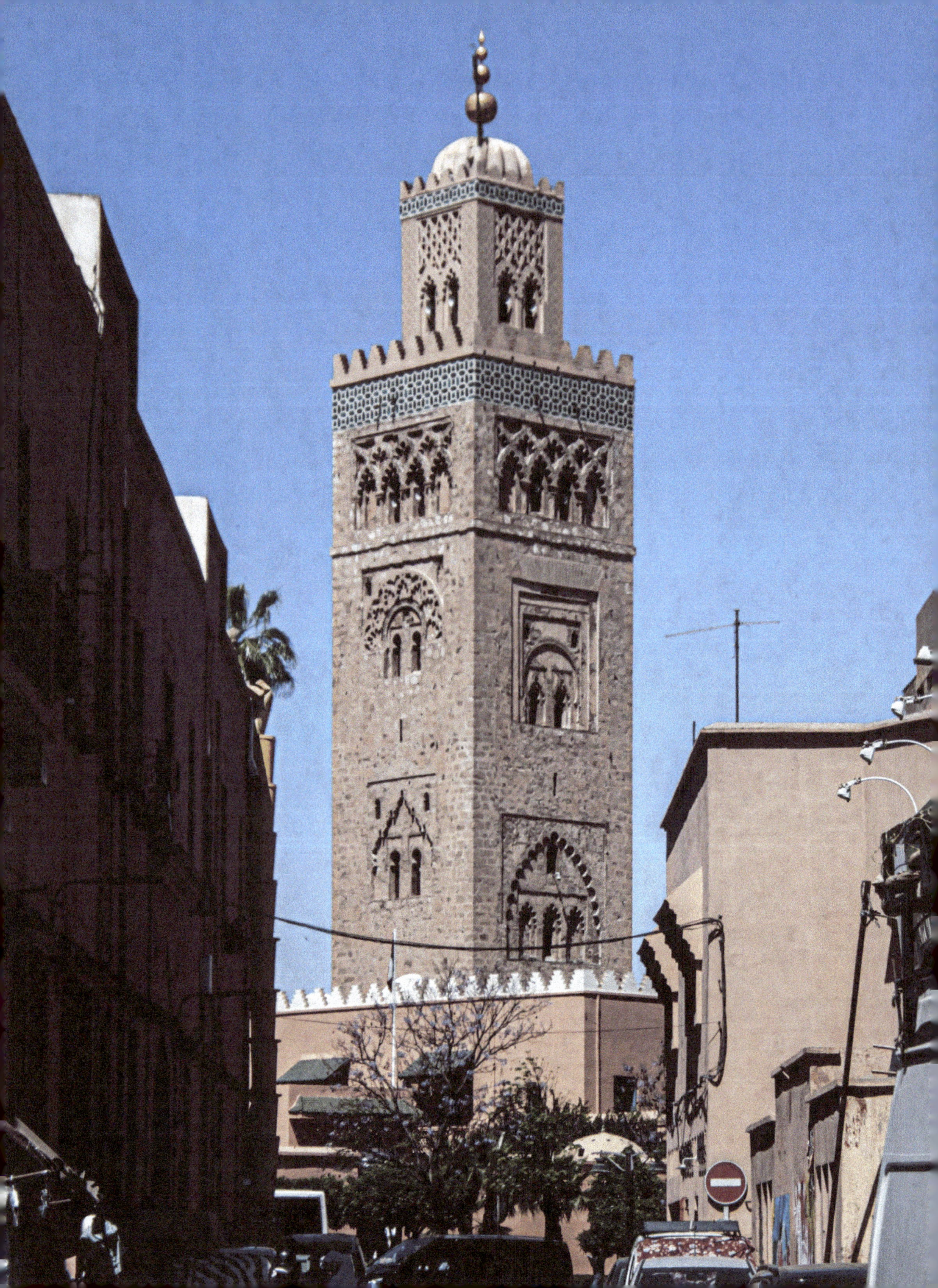

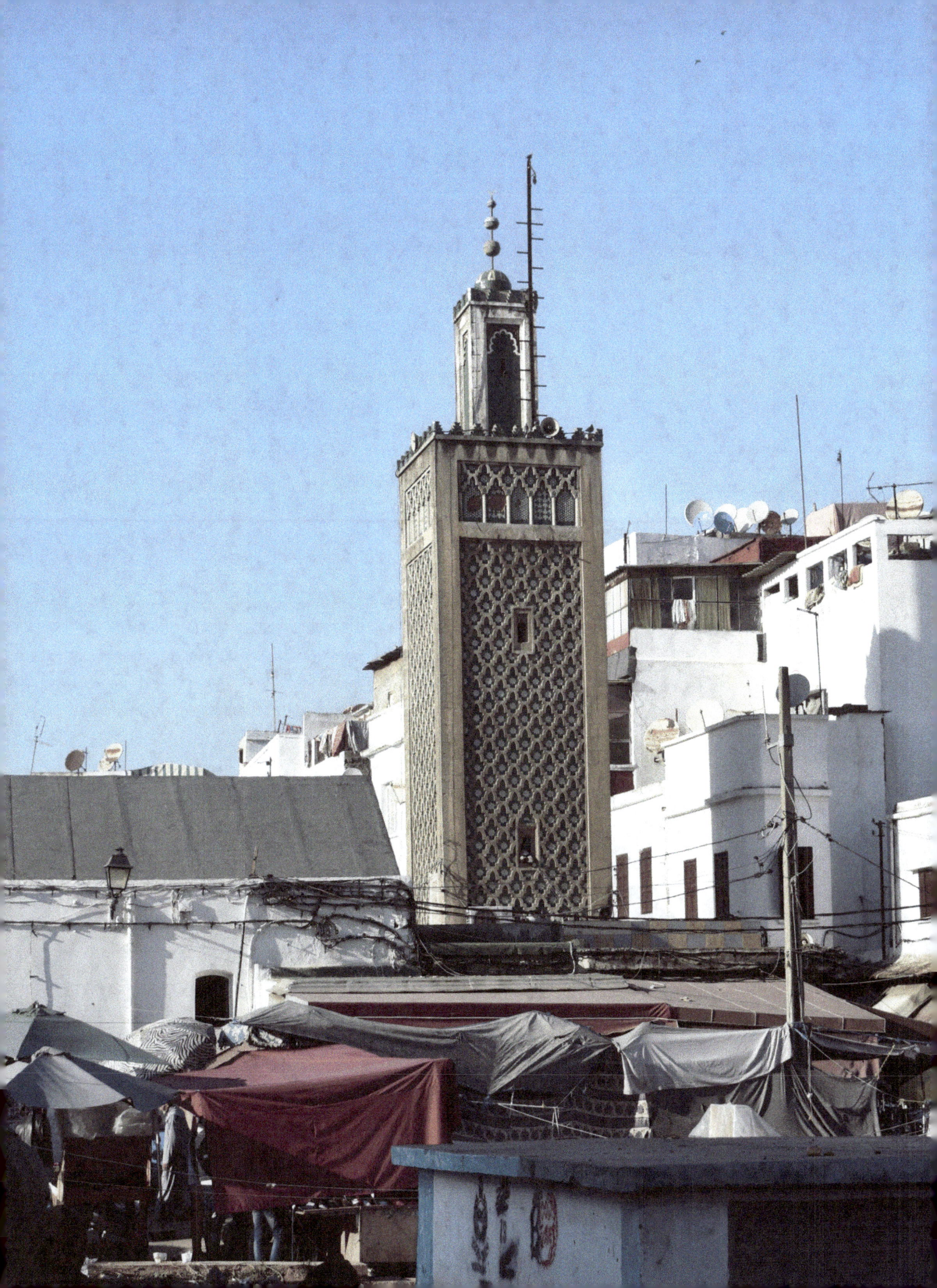

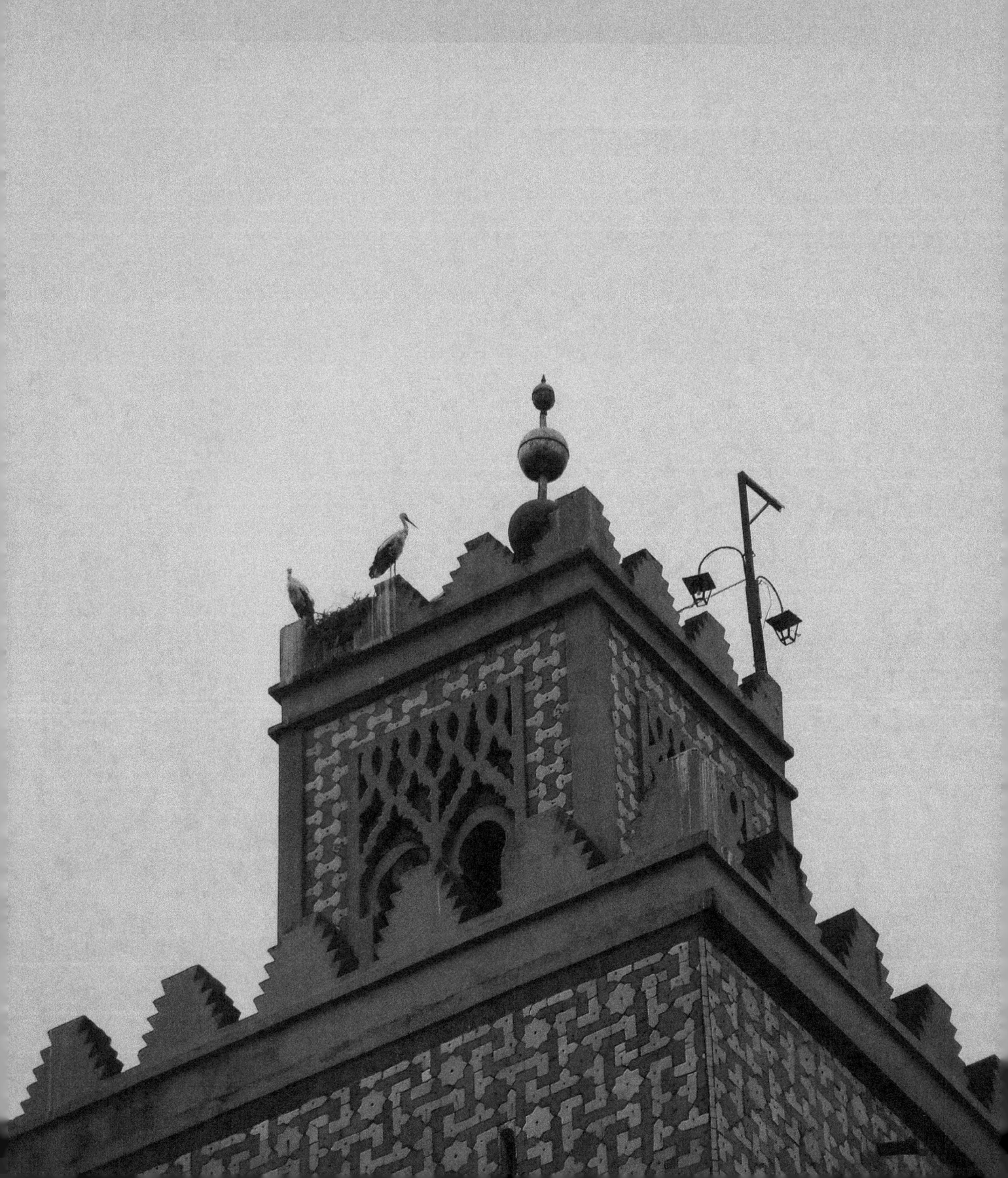

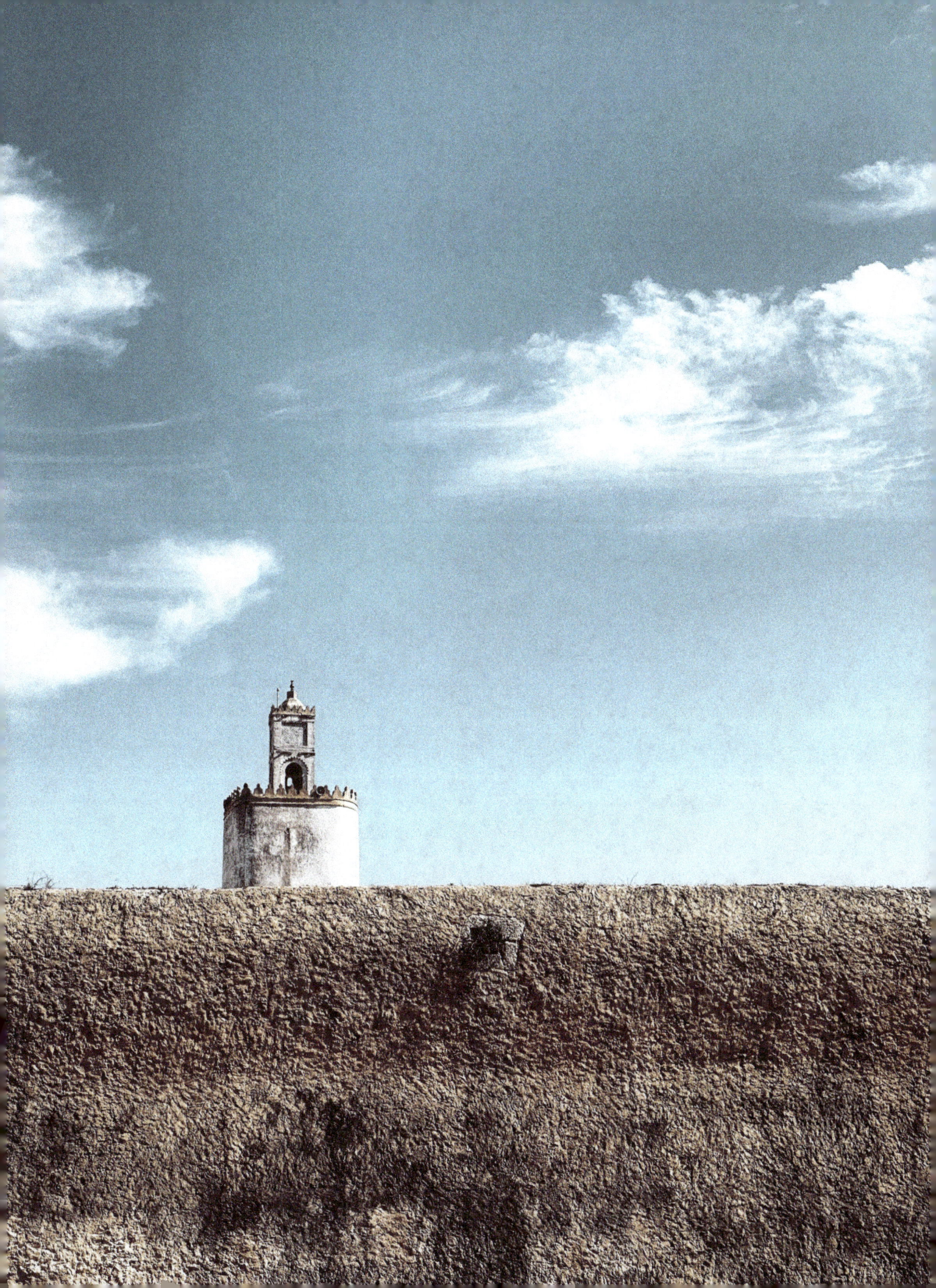

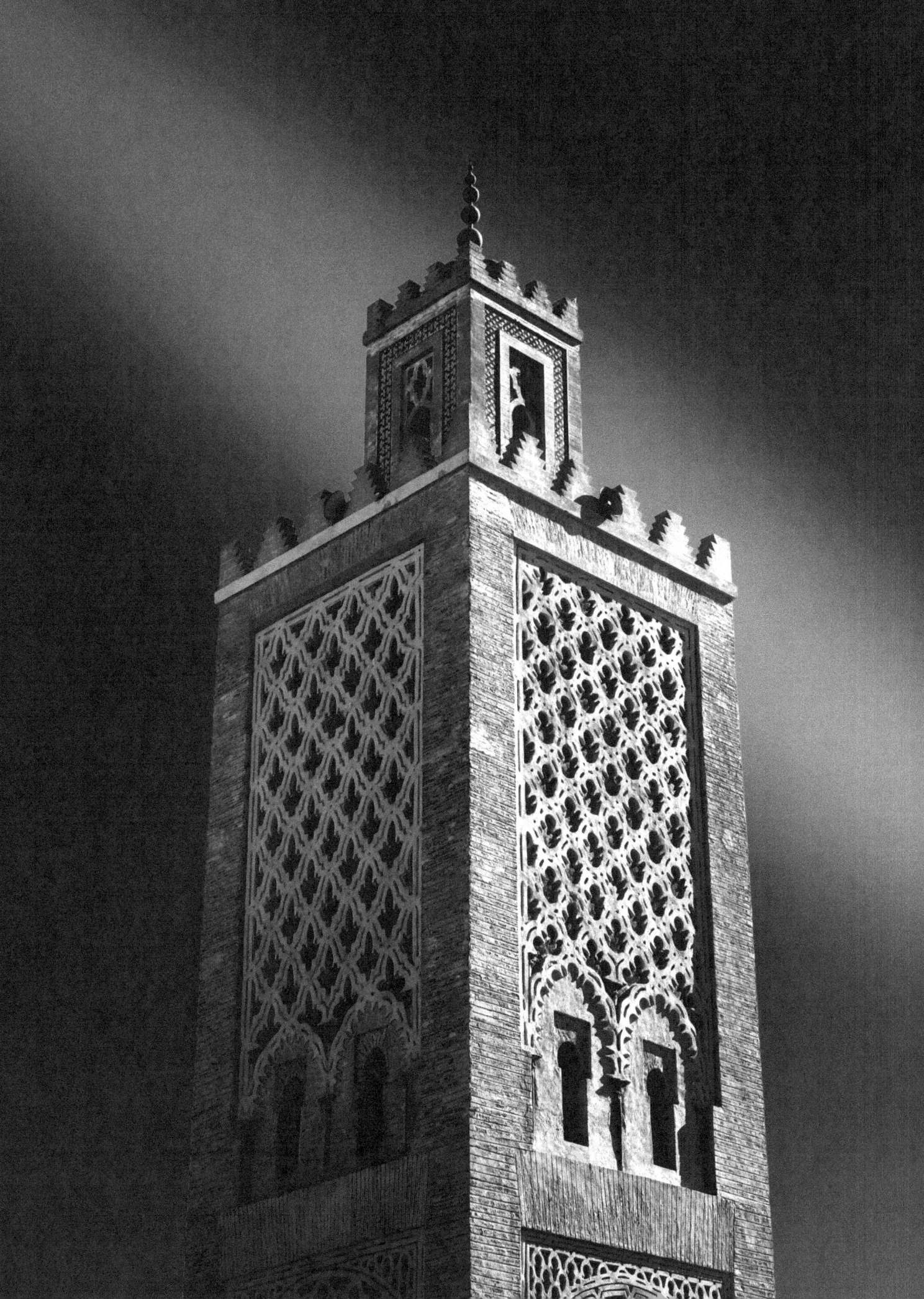

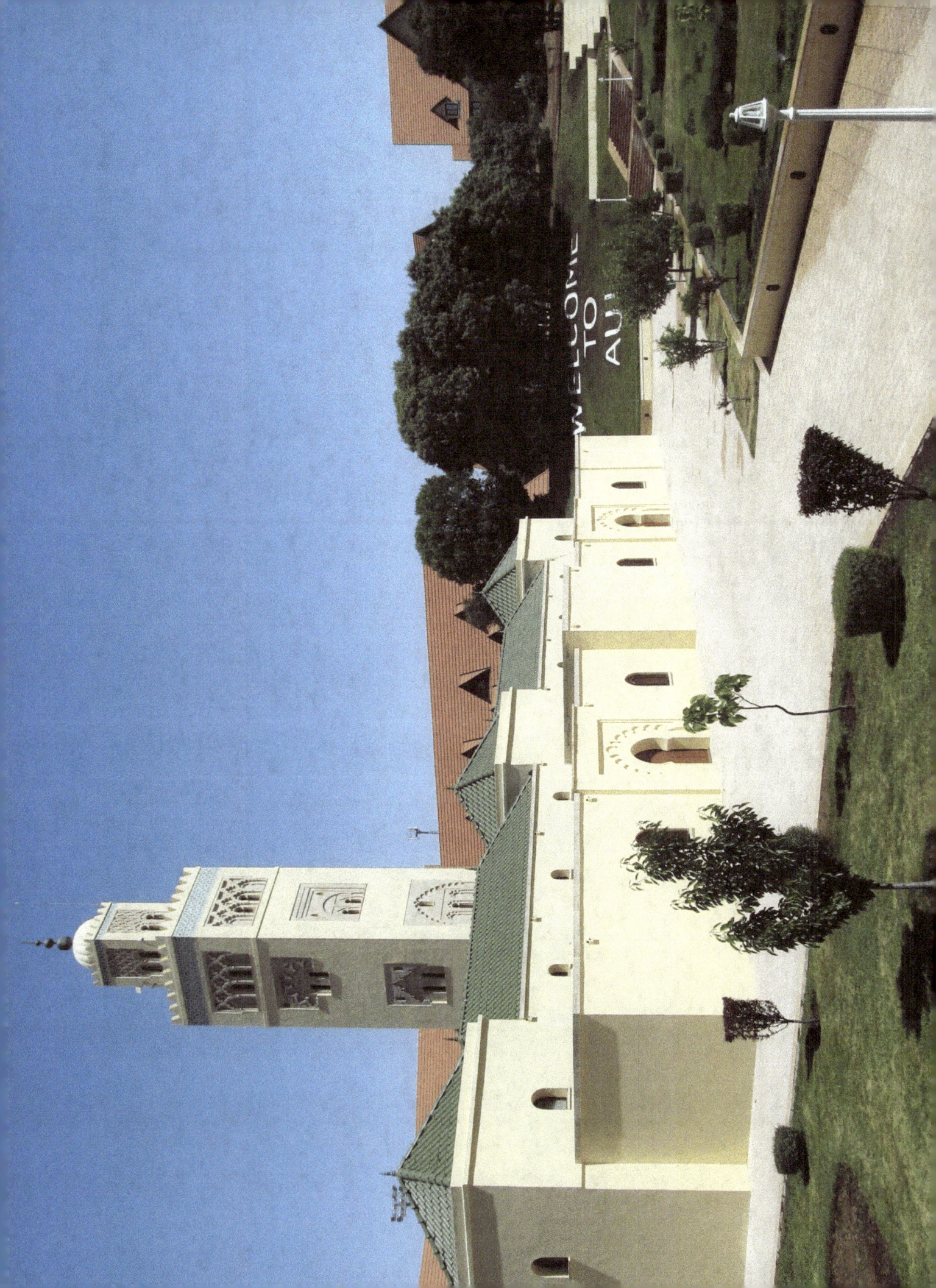

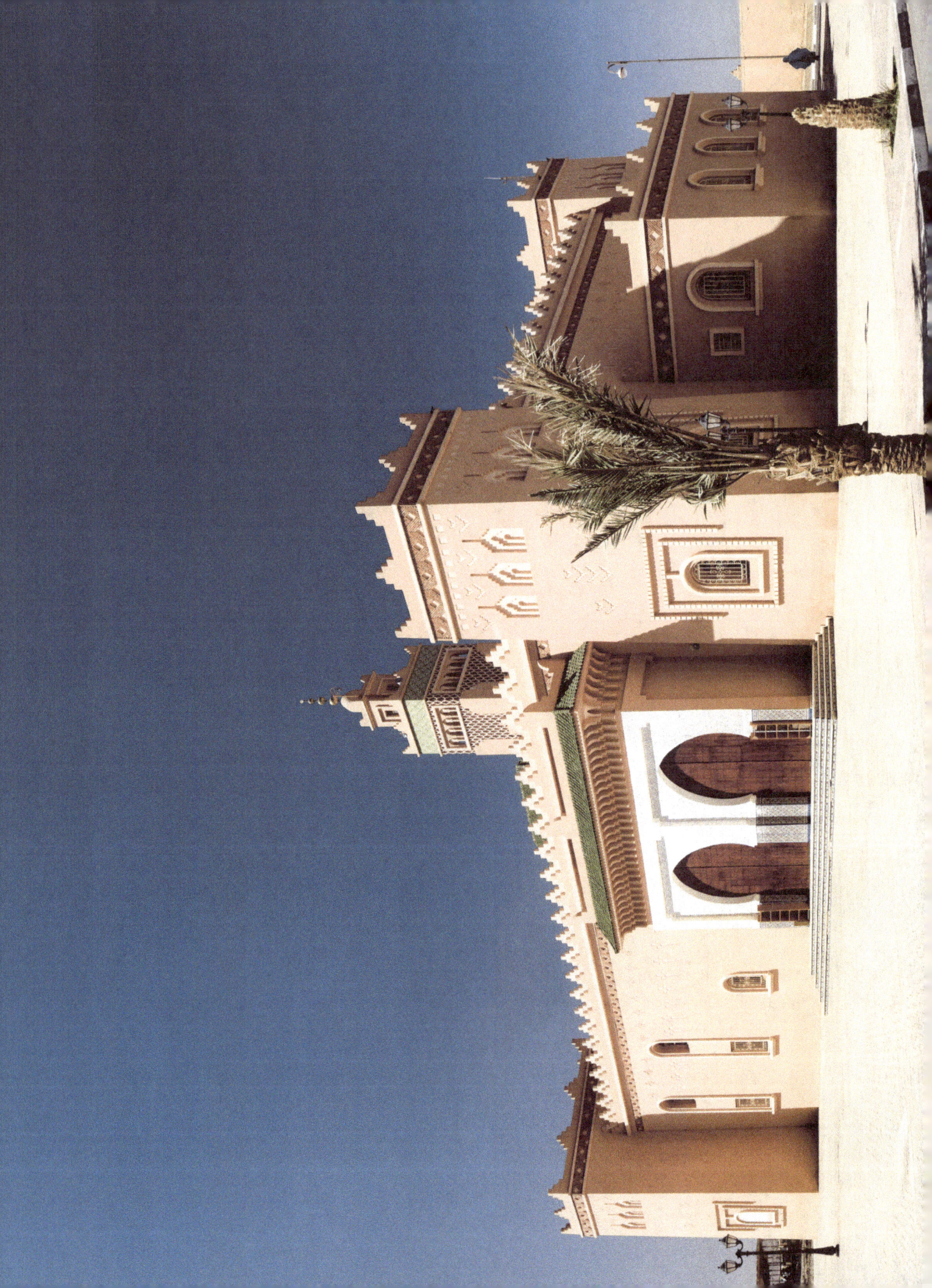

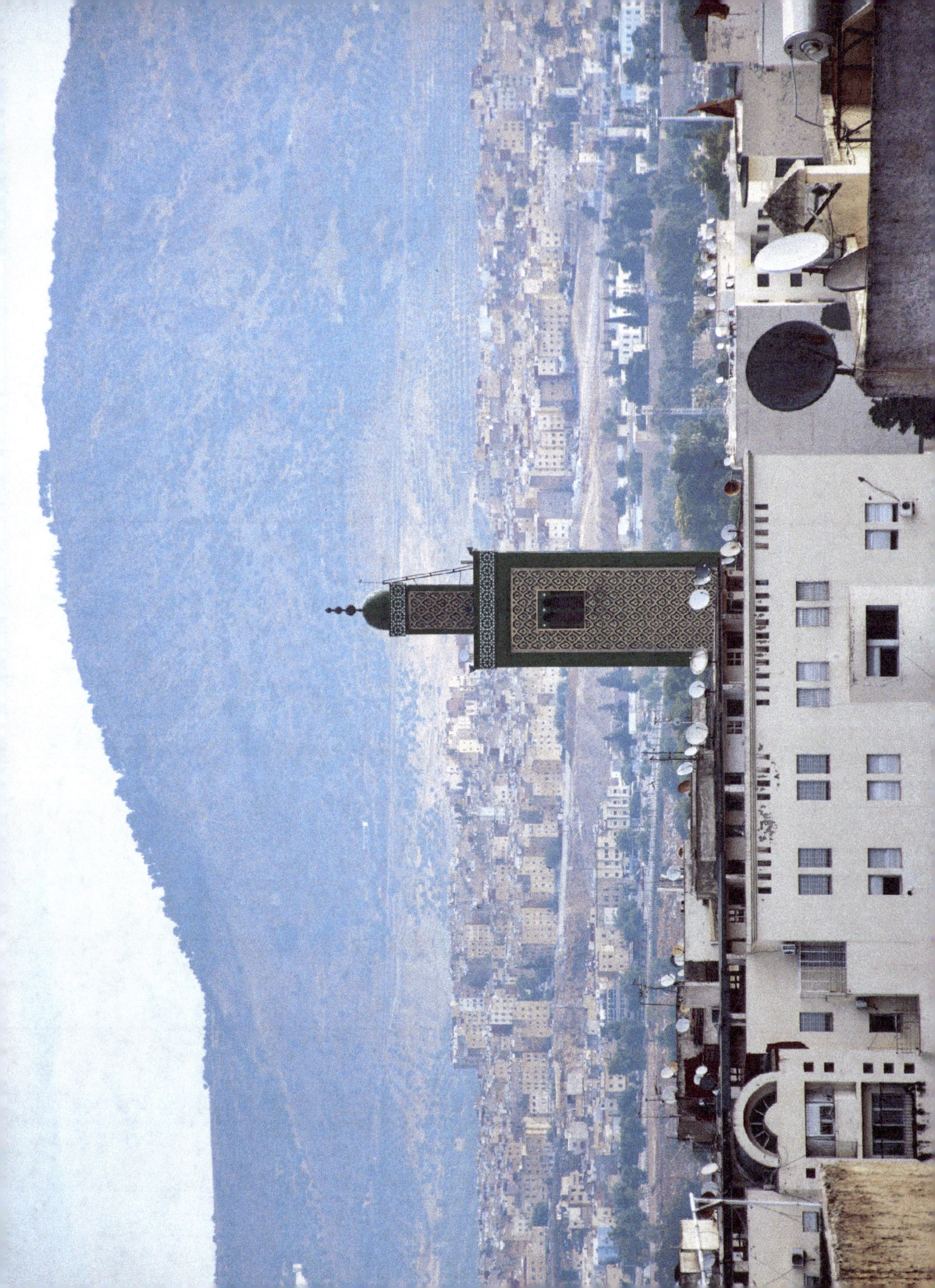

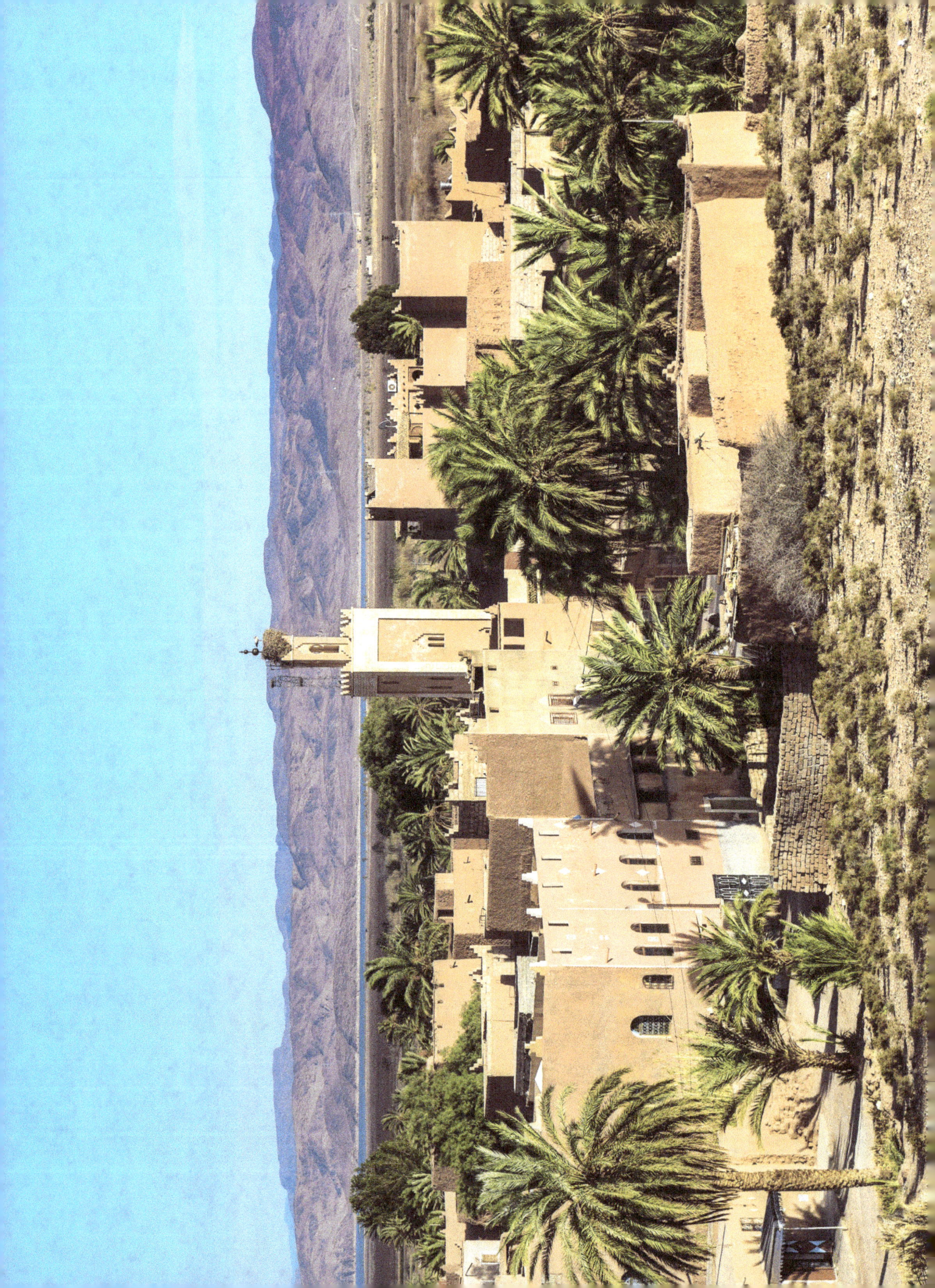

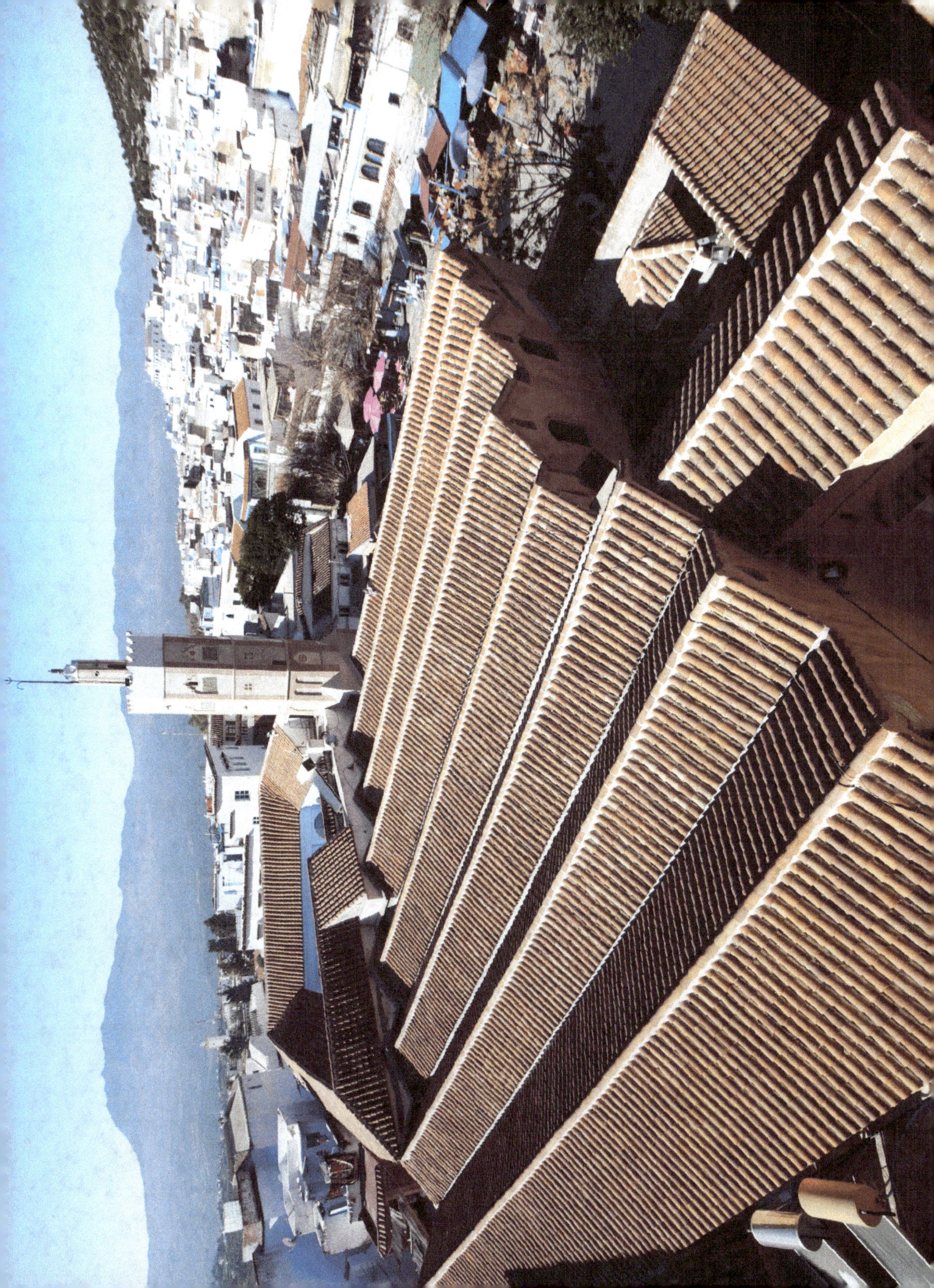

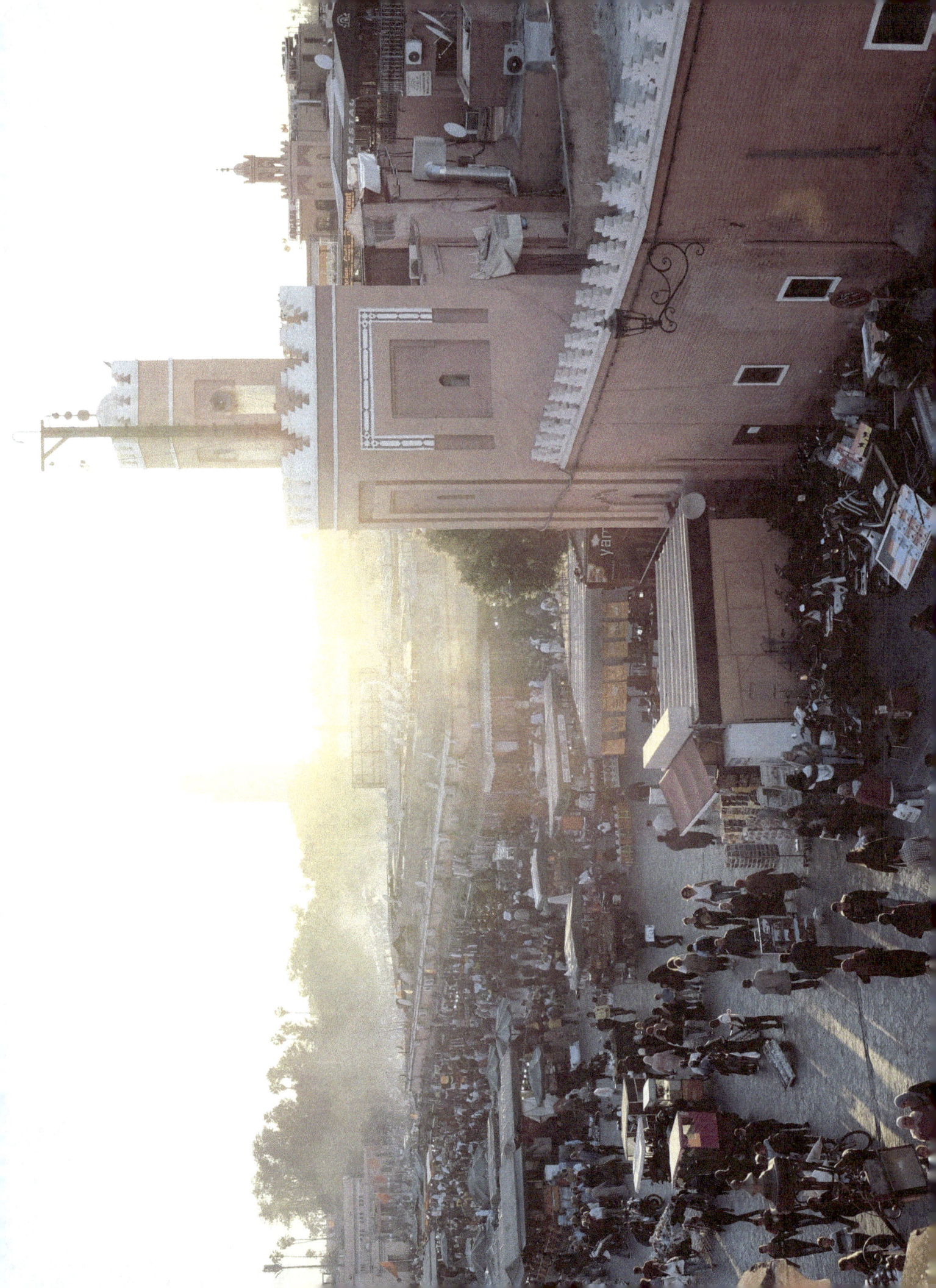

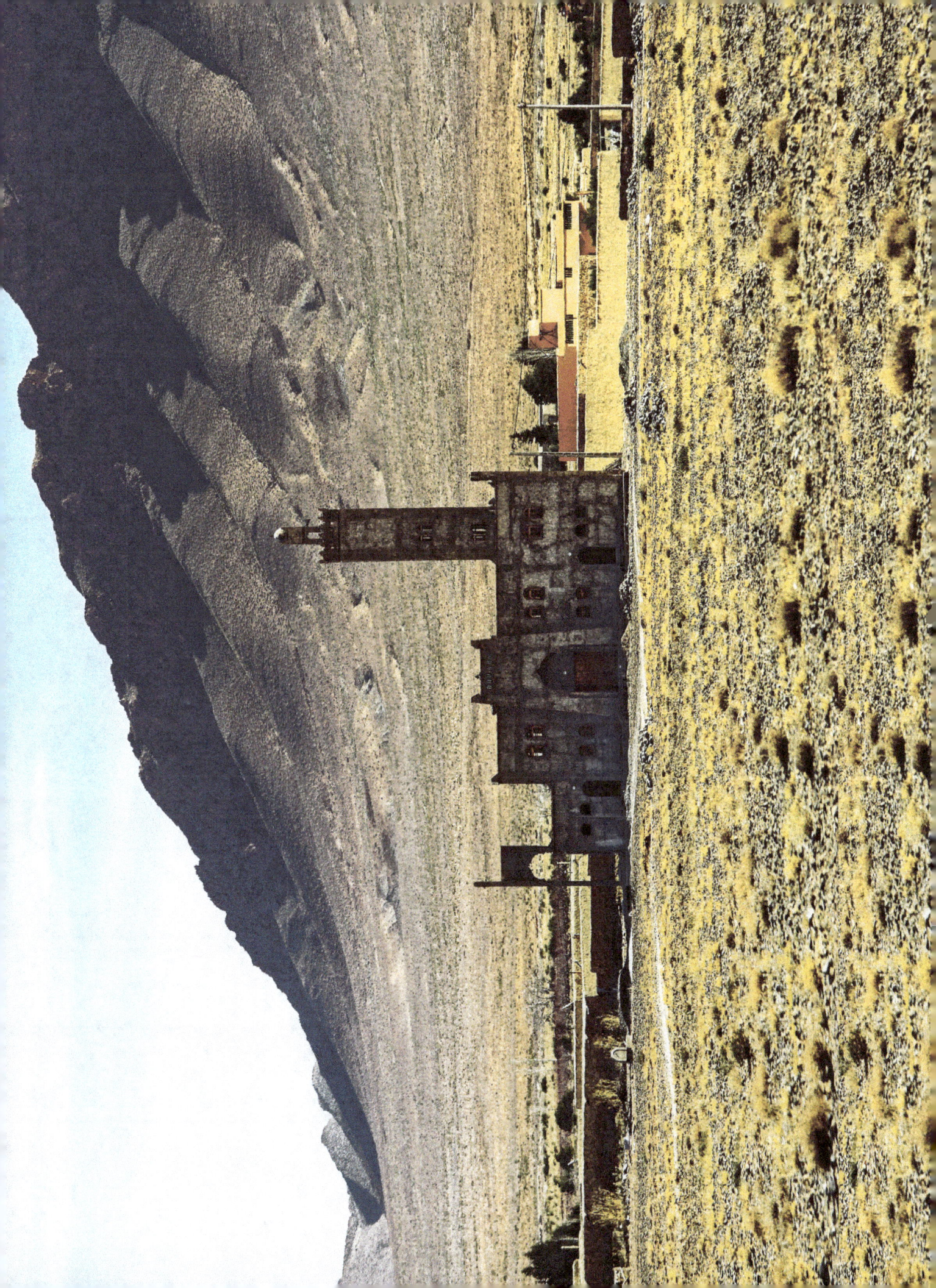

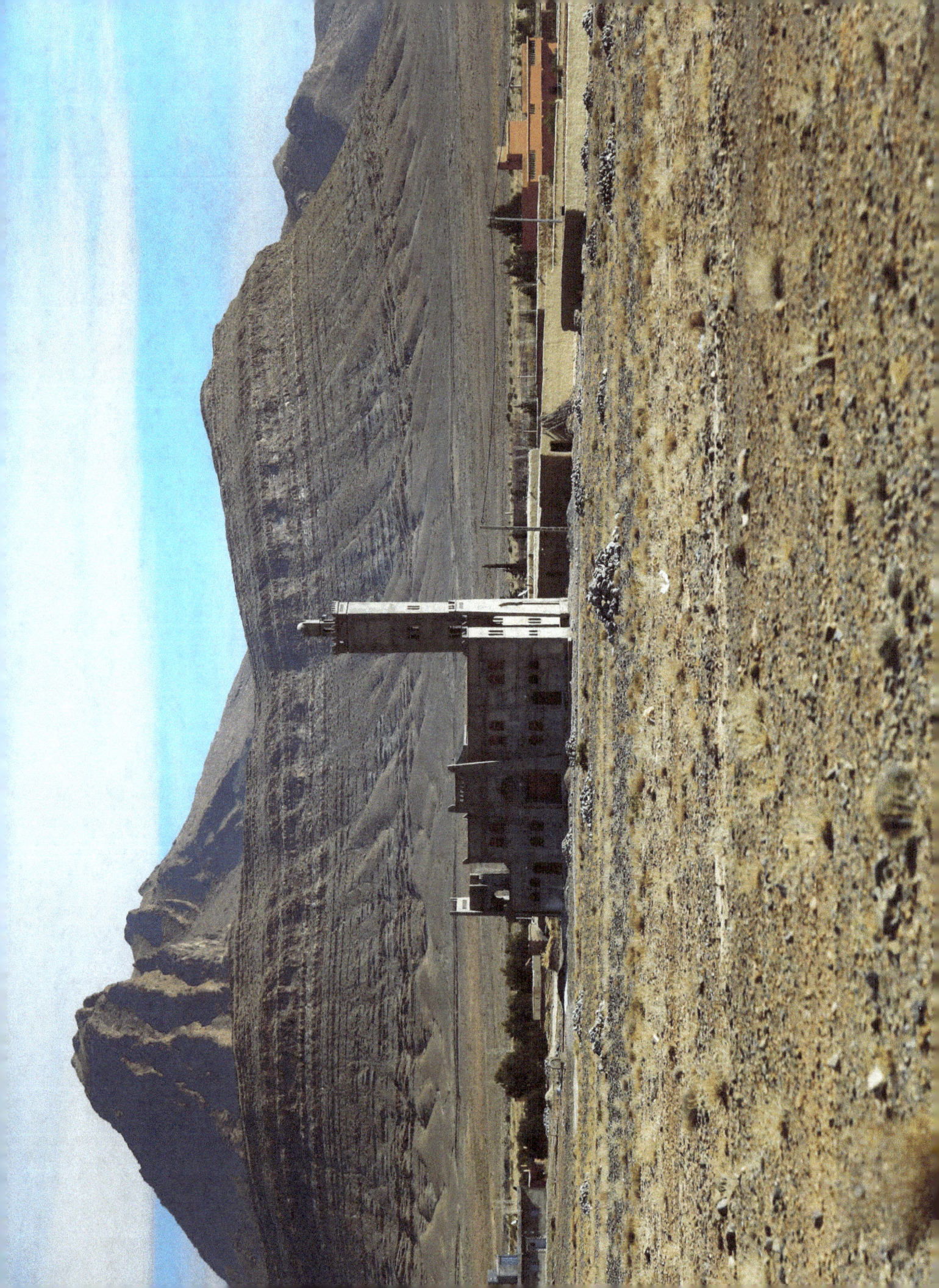

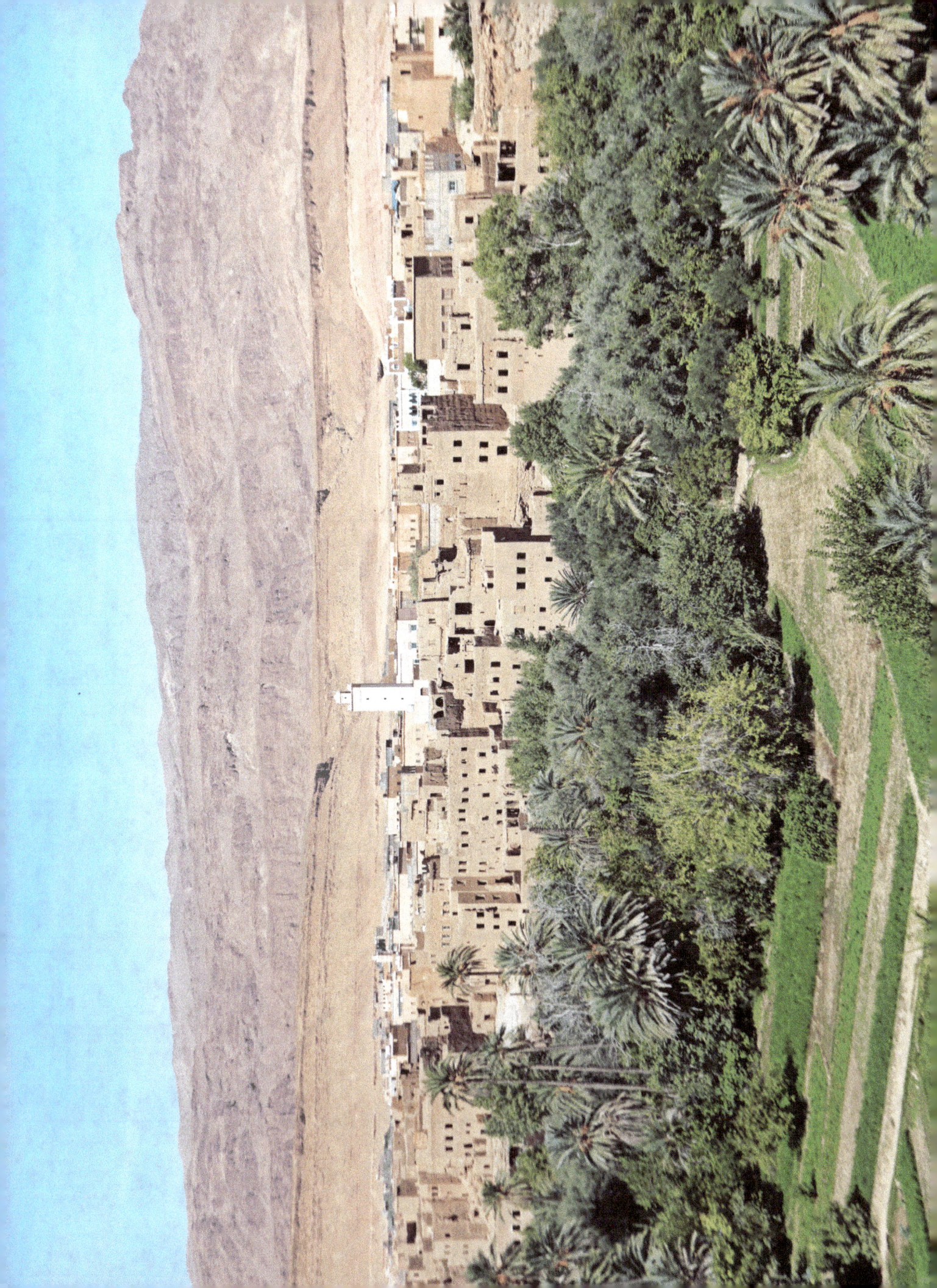

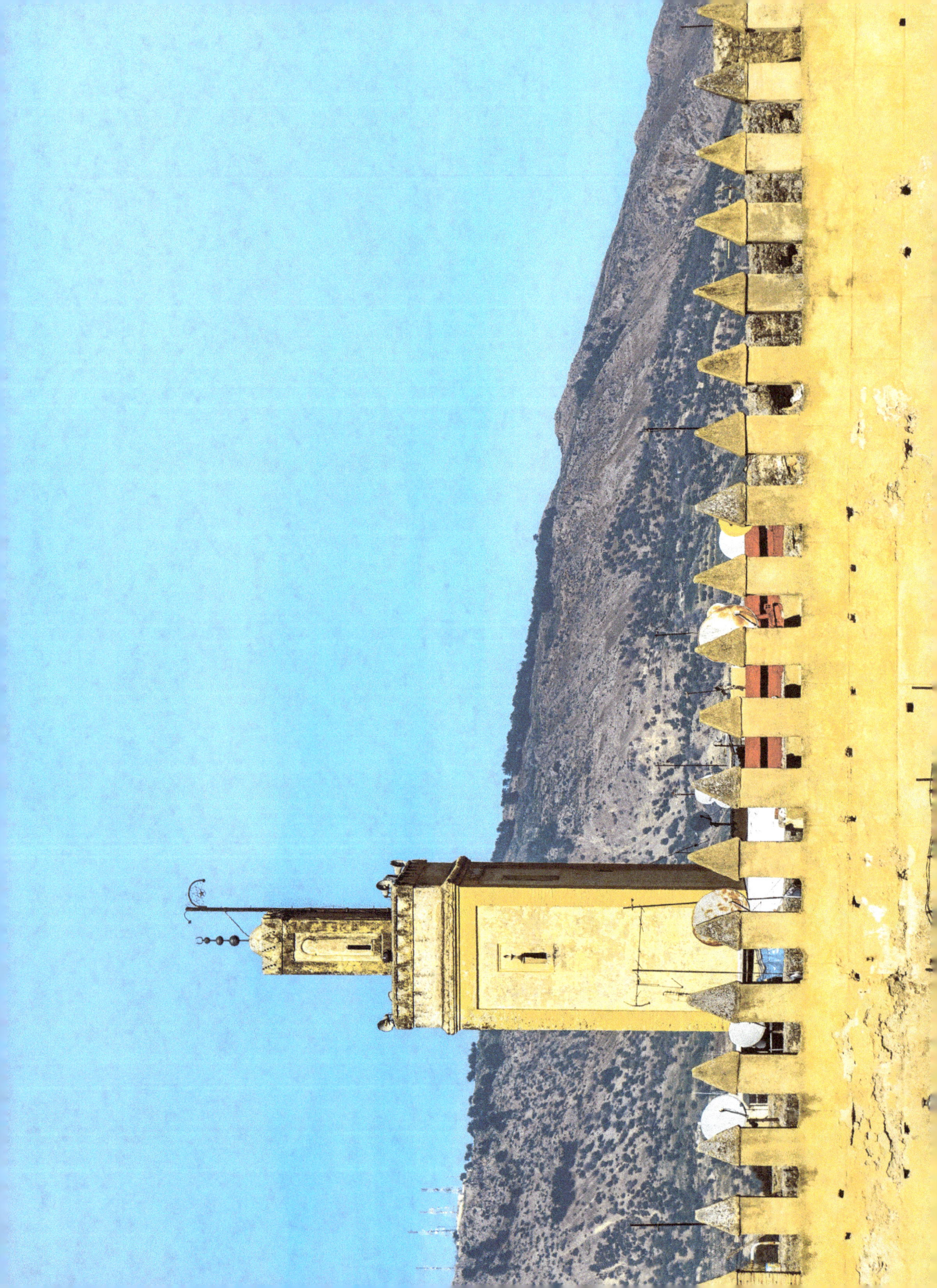

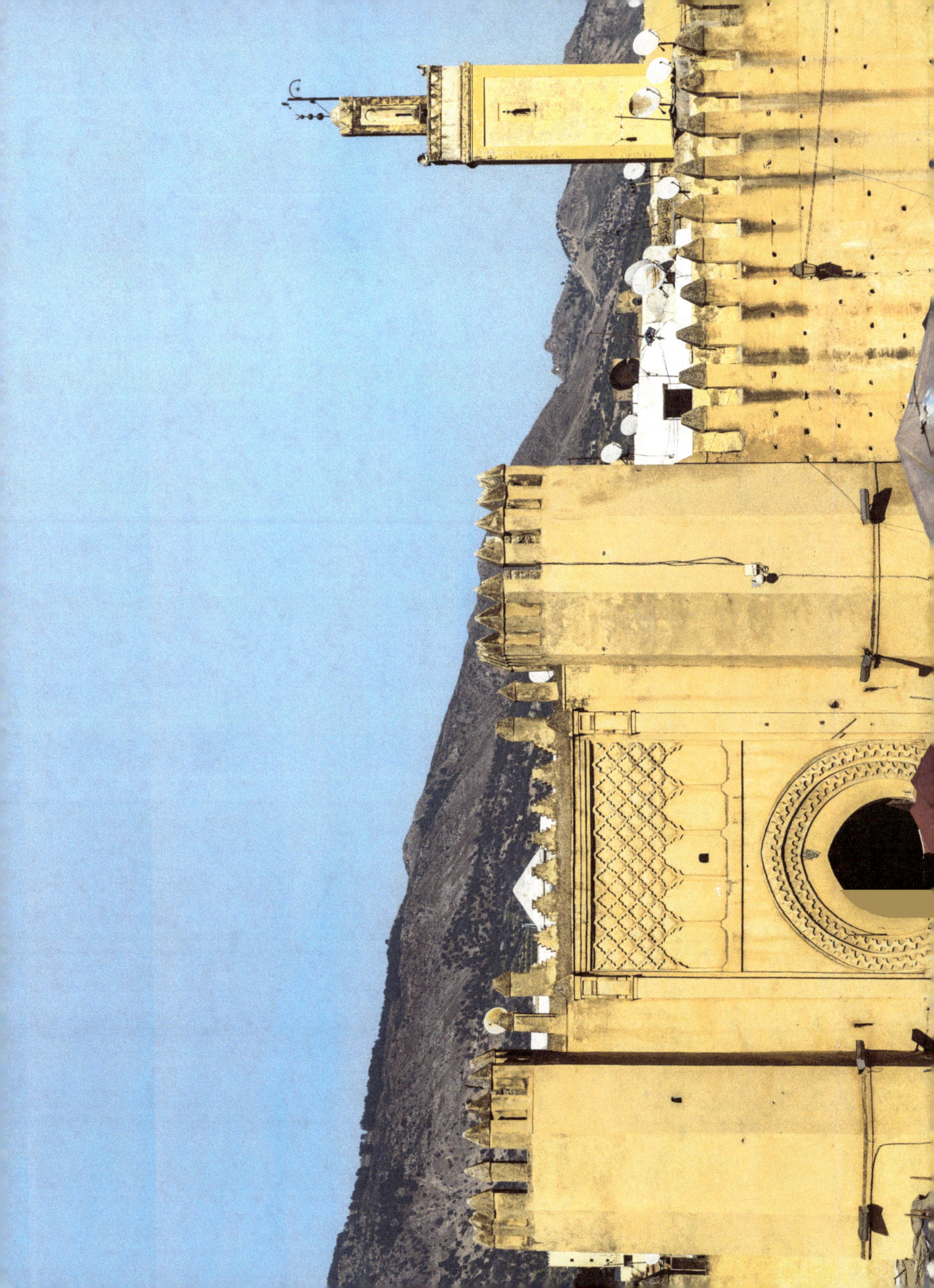

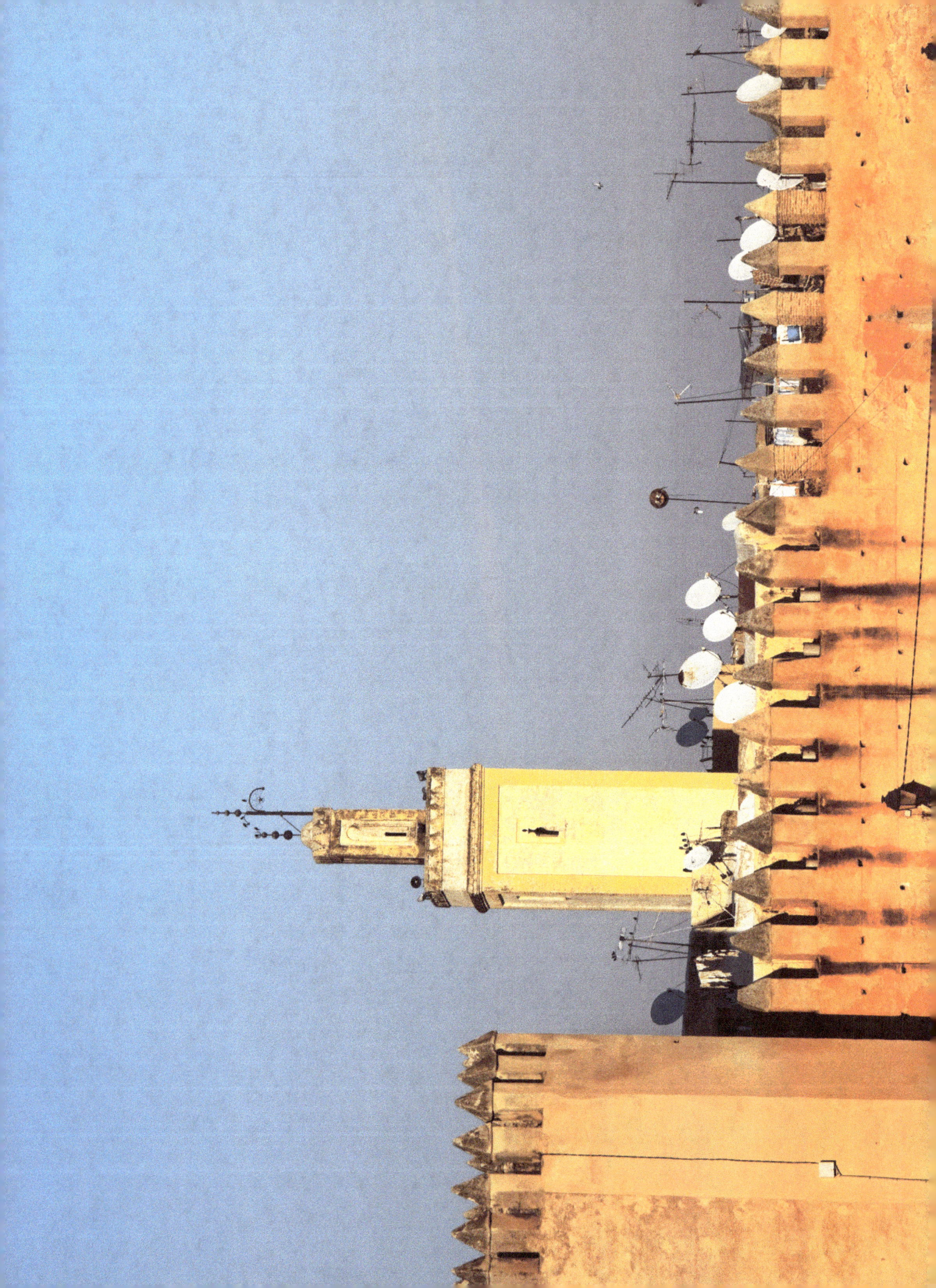

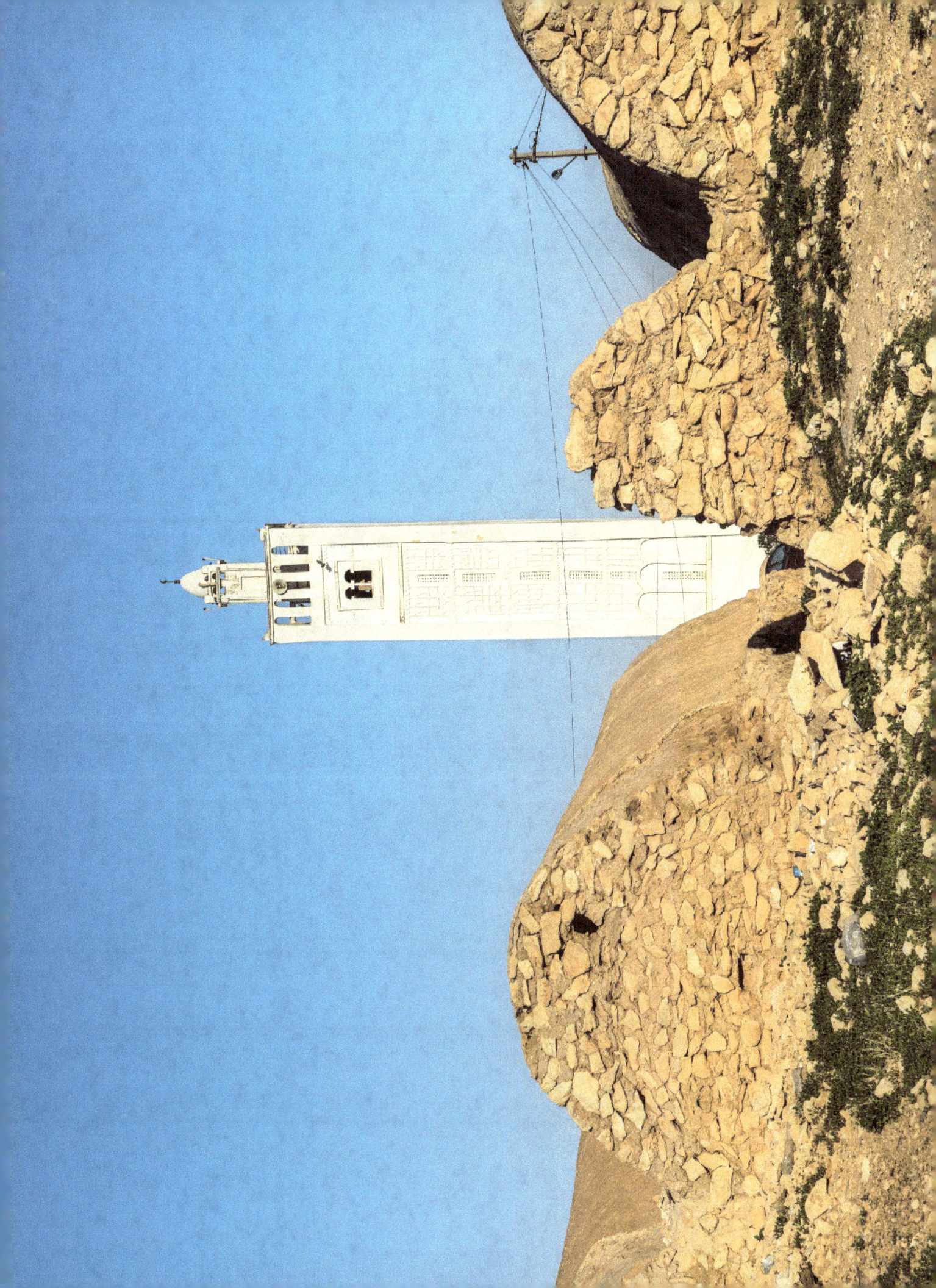

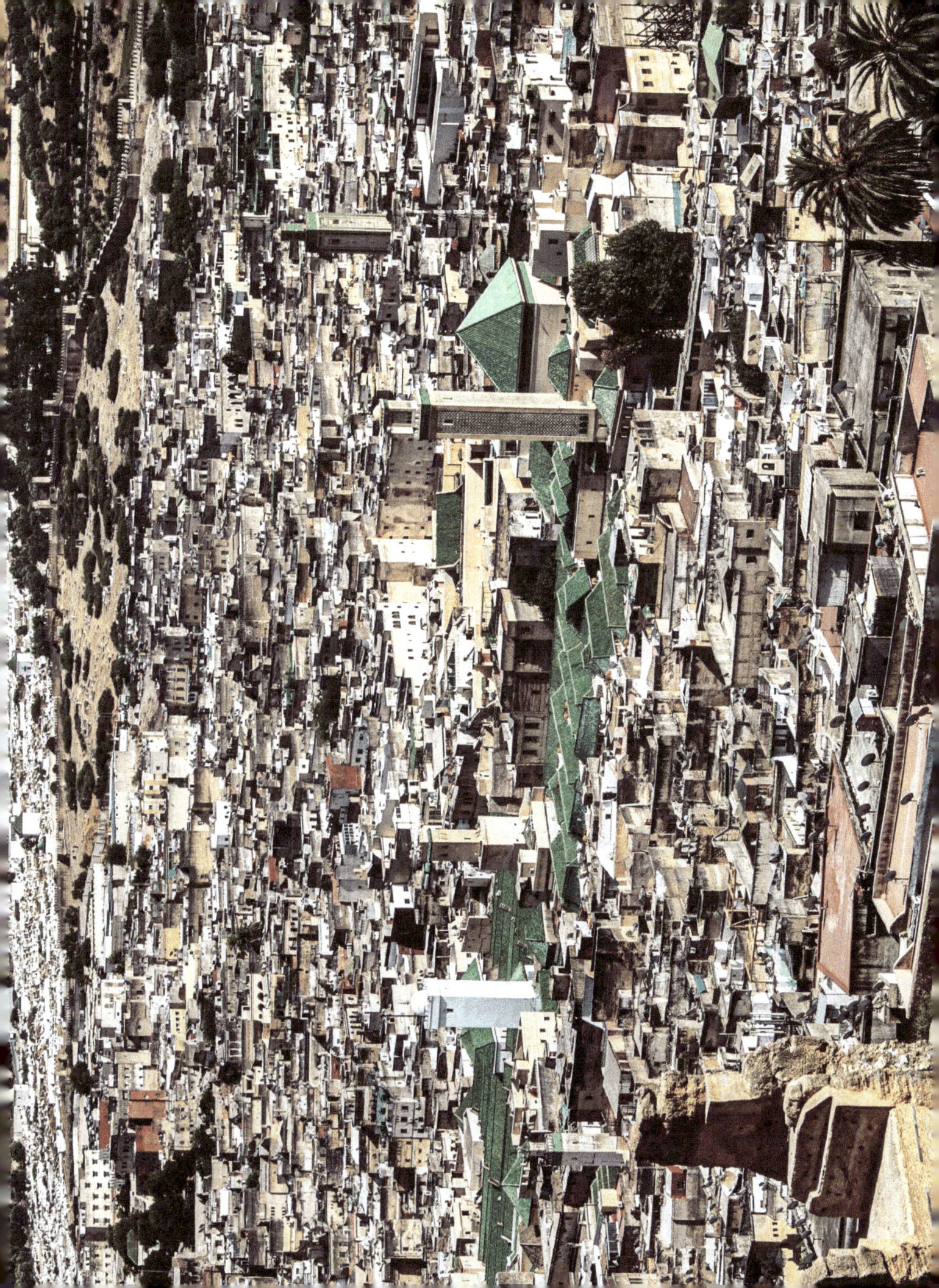

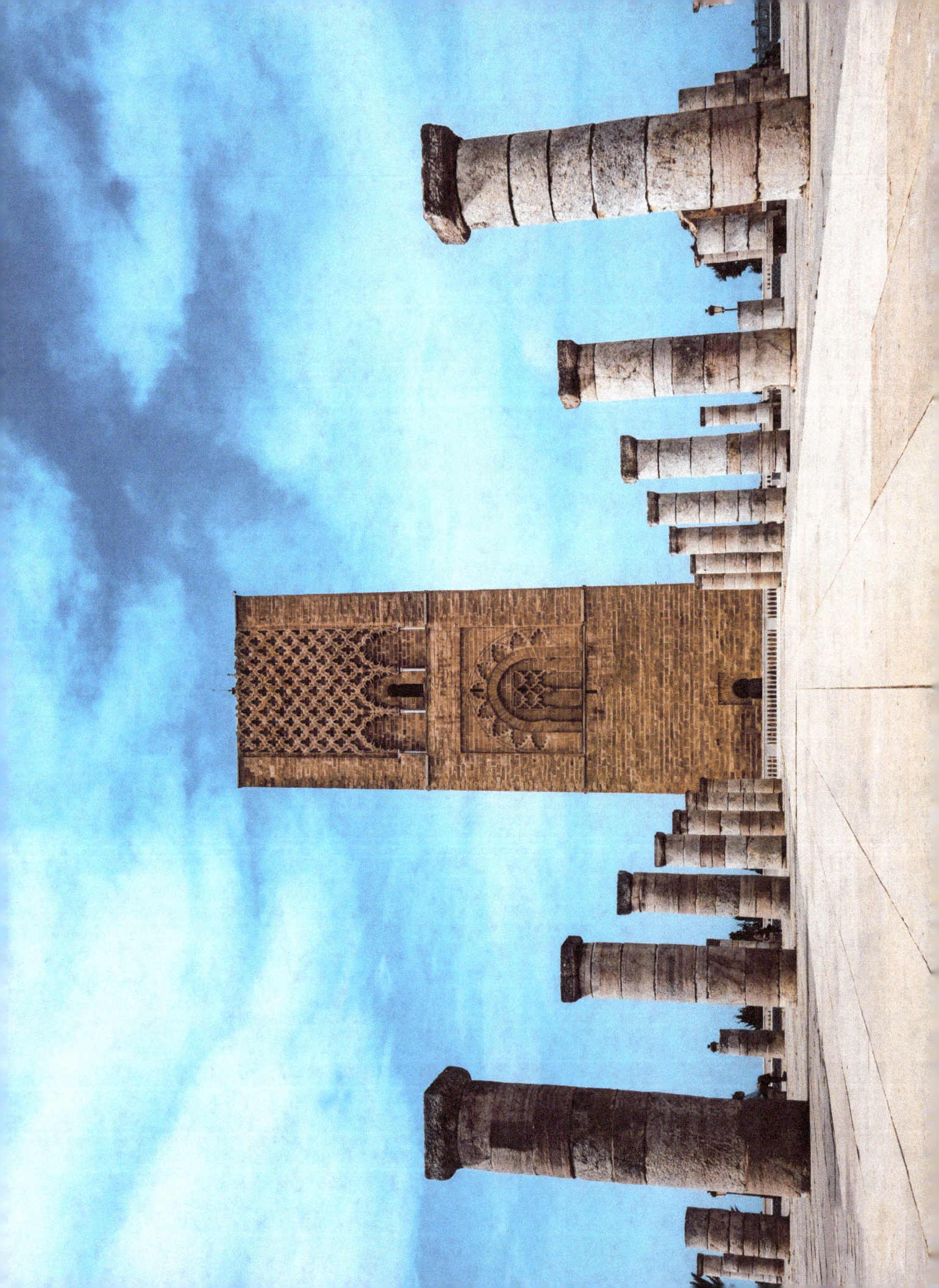

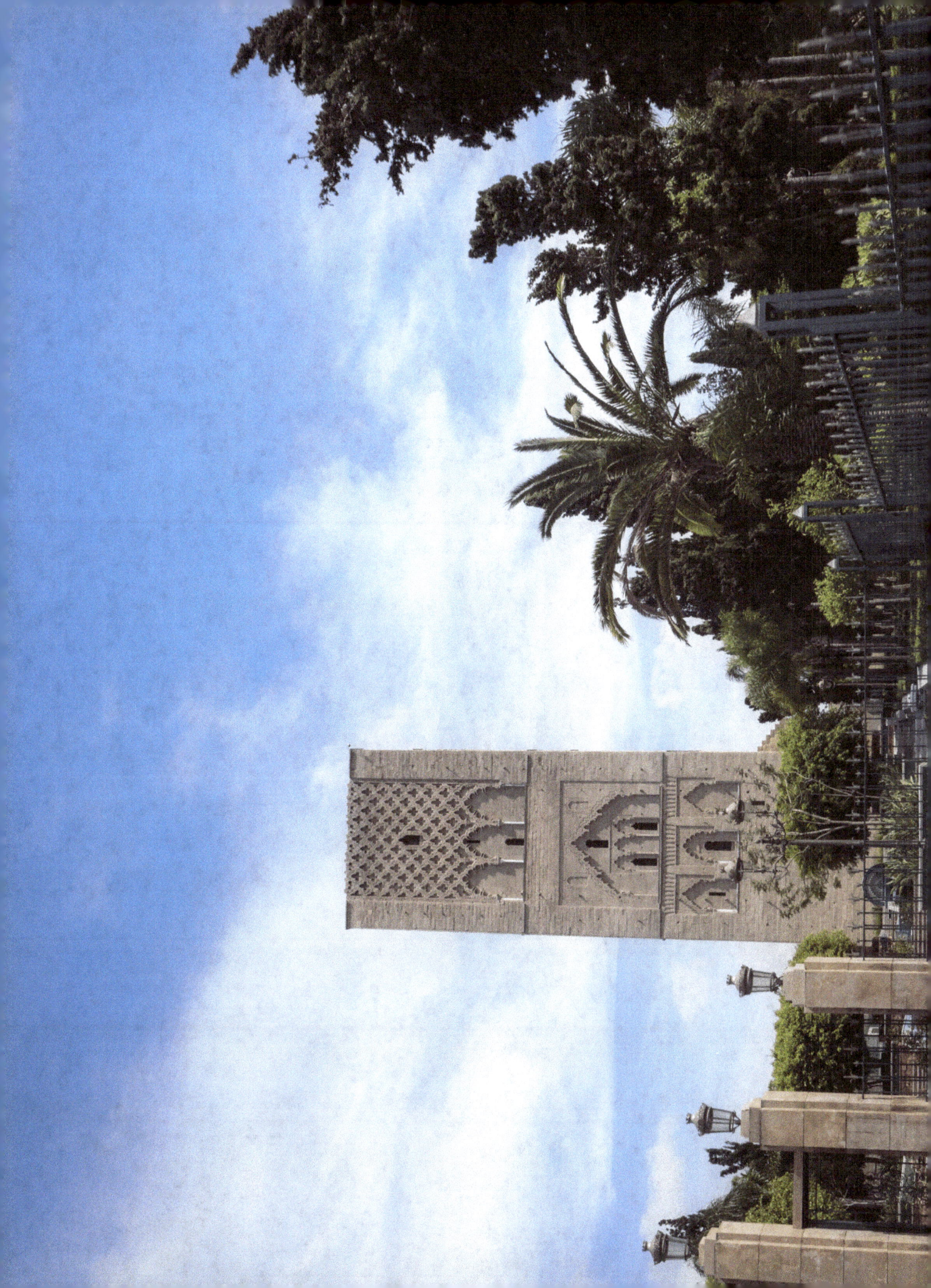

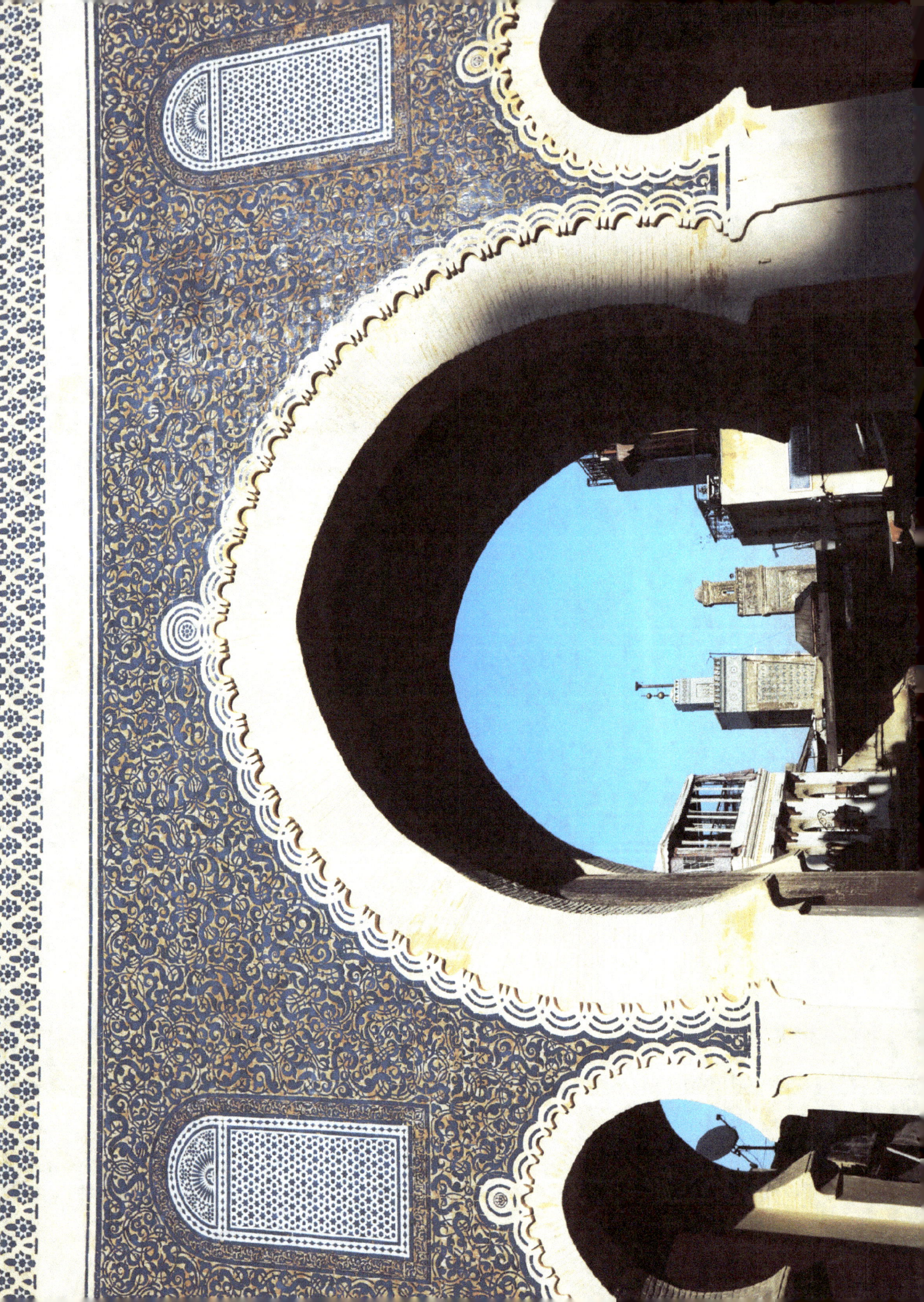

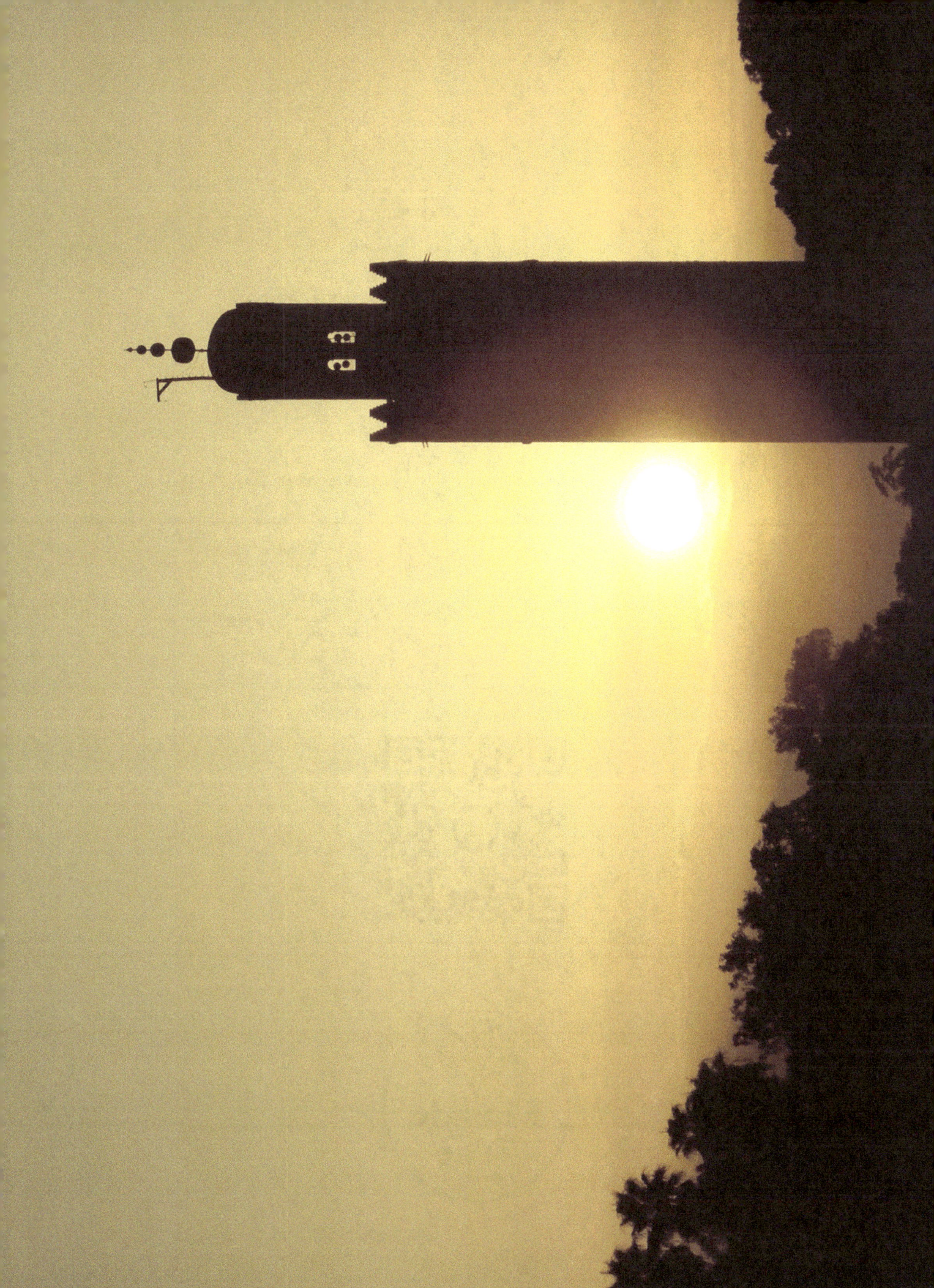

Browse our full catalogue at

MosaicTree.org

 Arabic Script & Sounds

 Arabic Vocabulary

 Arabic for Little Ones

 Arabic/Islamic Mosaic & Calligraphy

 Arabic Learning Journals

 Well-Being & Character Development

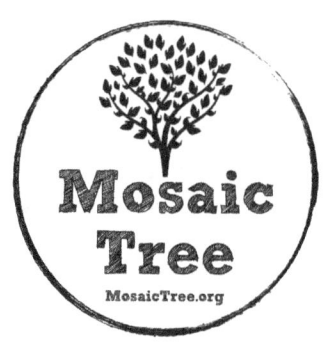

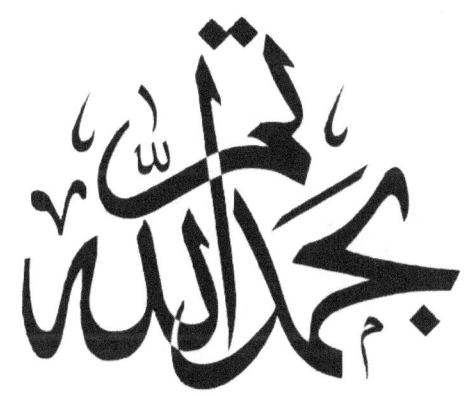

Completed with the grace of God

www.ingramcontent.com/pod-product-compliance
Lightning Source LLC
Chambersburg PA
CBHW082008230526

45468CB00023B/2836